PRAISE FOR
SECRETS OF THE KORAN

If one ignores the central message of this book, one does so
to one's own peril. Some have said "ignorance is bliss."
They are wrong. Ignorance can cost one dearly. And this applies
to the topic of Islam.

Whenever one discusses Islam, two choices are left: (1) speak the
truth and make some people very upset, or (2) sugarcoat the facts
and be quite popular. Don Richardson chose the former.
He is a truth speaker. This will not make him popular, but it
will make him historically correct on the issues. I have only
two more words to say about Don's book: read it.

DR. JIM GARLOW
AUTHOR, *A CHRISTIAN'S RESPONSE TO ISLAM*

Secrets of the Koran, written by one of the foremost missionary
statesmen of our day, is a timely book for all those who love the
truth. The same Jesus who "had to go through Samaria" (John 4:4)
went out of His way to minister to one woman (love) and then told
her, when she confidently referred Him to their place of worship,
"You Samaritans worship what you do not know" (v. 22) (truth).
Don Richardson's book will serve to educate Western Christians
and leaders about the truth concerning the Islamic religion
while maintaining the imperative of reaching
the Muslim masses with the gospel.

WALEED NASSAR
PRESIDENT, GREAT COMMISSION MINISTRIES INTERNATIONAL
WWW.GCMINTERNATIONAL.ORG

There is little doubt that a major obstacle to reaching unsaved
people in the world today is the dark spiritual power behind Islam
named Allah. The first step toward binding this "strong man"
is to understand what we are dealing with under the surface.
I know of no better place to start than Don Richardson's
powerful book *Secrets of the Koran.*

C. PETER WAGNER
CHANCELLOR, WAGNER LEADERSHIP INSTITUTE

SECRETS
OF THE
KORAN

DON RICHARDSON

Regal

From Gospel Light
Ventura, California, U.S.A.

PUBLISHED BY REGAL BOOKS
FROM GOSPEL LIGHT
VENTURA, CALIFORNIA, U.S.A.
Regal PRINTED IN THE U.S.A.

Regal Books is a ministry of Gospel Light, an evangelical Christian publisher dedicated to serving the local church. We believe God's vision for Gospel Light is to provide church leaders with biblical, user-friendly materials that will help them evangelize, disciple and minister to children, youth and families.

It is our prayer that this Regal book will help you discover biblical truth for your own life and help you meet the needs of others. May God richly bless you.

For a free catalog of resources from Regal Books/Gospel Light, please call your Christian supplier or contact us at 1-800-4-GOSPEL *or* www.regalbooks.com.

Library of Congress Cataloging-in-Publication Data

Richardson, Don, 1935-
   Secrets of the Koran : revealing insight into Islam's holy book / Don Richardson.
      p. cm.
Includes bibliographical references.
   ISBN 0-8307-3124-5 (hardcover)   ISBN 0-8307-3123-7 (paperback)
   1. Islam—Controversial literature. 2. Koran—Controversial
literature. 3. Koran—Criticism, interpretation, etc. 4. Islam—Relations—Christianity.
5. Christianity and other
religions—Islam. I. Title.
   BT1170 .R53 2003
   297—dc21   2002015991

2   3   4   5   6   7   8   9   10   11   12   13   14   15   /   09   08   07   06   05   04   03

Any omission of credits is unintentional. The publisher requests documentation for future printings.

Rights for publishing this book in other languages are contracted by Gospel Light Worldwide, the international nonprofit ministry of Gospel Light. Gospel Light Worldwide also provides publishing and technical assistance to international publishers dedicated to producing Sunday School and Vacation Bible School curricula and books in the languages of the world. For additional information, visit www.gospellightworldwide.org; write to Gospel Light Worldwide, P.O. Box 3875, Ventura, CA 93006; or send an e-mail to info@gospellightworldwide.org.

CONTENTS

FOREWORD

On September 11, 2001, the world took a major turn. In the spiritual realm, a demonic force made a new declaration of its existence, purpose and resolve. In the natural realm, the free world faced a new challenge threatening its very survival. This so-called faceless enemy is not a philosophy, such as communism, but one that has a fearful theological ideology that has penetrated, to one degree or another, the hearts of 1.2 billion people around the world.

In the political arena there are always compromises because of the nature of the system. Truth can be a relative issue depending upon whom it will benefit. For example, after September 11, politicians and news reporters declared that Islam is a peaceful religion and that groups such as al-Qaeda are just the fanatical offbeat type that do not represent true Islam. Few ask upon what basis their assessment is made. Are politicians and reporters relying upon their personal knowledge of the teaching and the traditions of Mohammed, the most holy prophet of Islam? Or are they relying upon the teaching of the most holy script of Islam, the Koran? Or the 1,400-year history of Islam?

In the United States, our judicial system is based upon facts, not hearsay, emotions, feelings or think sos! In other words, we—as jury members in the court of public opinion—cannot base our assessment of the intentions of a religion with which we are unfamiliar upon the opinions of our political analysts. We must have facts because the lives of millions of people depend upon our assessment.

If Islam is a peaceful religion, then why did Mohammed engage in 47 battles? Why, in every campaign the Muslim armies have fought throughout history, have they slaughtered men, women and children who did not bow their knees to the lordship of Islam? The reign of terror of men such as Saddam, Khomeini, Ghadafi, Idi Amin and many other Muslim dictators are modern examples. If Islam is peaceful, why are there so many verses in the Koran about killing the infidels and those who resist Islam? If Islam is peaceful, why isn't there even one Muslim country that will allow freedom of religion and speech? Not one! If Islam is peaceful, who is imparting this awful violence to hundreds of Islamic groups throughout the world who kill innocent people in the name of Allah?

The undeniable truth is recorded in the history of what Mohammed did in his lifetime and what, as laid out in the Koran, the god of Islam requires of his followers. The Islam that Mohammed proclaimed in the seventh century is something for all of us to take a closer look at because that version of Islam is more violent and has more resolve than many might think.

Seventh-century Islamic despotism continued until the fall of the Ottoman Empire, then lay relatively dormant for a season. But since the statehood of Israel was established in 1948, the Islam of Mohammed of the seventh century has been on the rise. It showed its capability and its nature with the revolution of the Ayatollah Khomeini in 1978 in Iran. And ever since, men such as Ghadafi and Osama bin Laden have been blowing the dust off the sword of a forceful world-invading religion—this true Islam is on the rise. The question is how do we deal with it?

We must know the truth even if it may be offensive. It is our only remedy to sustain freedom and peace. If our processing of the truth about Islam causes more Muslims to be mad at us, do we compromise and back off from the truth for the sake of not being offensive, or do we proceed? We must, in my opinion, proceed, because the lie is more harmful. Do you stop your child from drinking a poisonous liquid, even if by doing so you may hurt his or her feelings? Obviously! Then why can't we look at the history of Islam, the teaching of the Koran and the life of Mohammed to find out if this religion is what politicians and reporters declare or if it is bent more toward what bin Laden practices? If bin Laden's version is true Islam, and if it is on the rise, I believe, the American people and the Western world have the right to know what is ahead and how to deal with it.

The challenge is to speak this truth in love. Our goal is not to be destructive but instructive. We should not yell at the darkness and the people who are bound by it, but rather open a door and let the light in. Don Richardson has done just that in this book, *Secrets of the Koran*. I pray that the Lord may raise more voices such as Don's, who can speak the truth in love. We must know the truth. The truth is our only path to freedom. Millions of Muslims around the world long for freedom, and they cannot be free unless more and more voices speak out the truth and expose the nature of a religion that has for centuries held its adherents in fear and bondage.

Then you will know the truth, and the truth will set you free (John 8:32).

A servant of Jesus Christ and an ex-Shiite radical Muslim,
Reza F. Safa

PREFACE

Every quote I use from the Koran has been compared with eight English translations, lest one translator's error would cause me to misread Mohammed's intent. Throughout this book I place direct quotes from the Koran in **bold** and citations from the Holy Bible in *italics*, so it is easy to tell which is which. I have chosen to use N. J. Dawood's English translation of the Koran as my primary text, but also quote from others as noted.

Various translations of the Koran differ slightly in how they *name* the chapters and how they *number* the verses. Thus it is best to focus on chapter *numbers* rather than the seemingly arbitrarily assigned names. Verse numbering in certain translations sometimes differs by one to three points. If the number I give for a particular verse does not correspond to what you find, look a little ahead or a little behind and you will find it.

In order to grasp the full original meaning of the Koranic text, I have in places put clarifications in brackets. This added information does not change the meaning or intent of the Koran, rather it provides clarification and context. Because this information is in brackets and not put in bold face, you can easily tell the difference between the Koranic text and the clarifications.

Seven Versions of the Koran Studied for this Critique, Identified by Their Translator's Names

- Maulana Muhammad Ali (Columbus, OH: Lahore, Inc., USA, 1998); M. M. Ali adds comments numbered from 1 to 2,822.
- Ahmed Ali (Princeton, NJ: Princeton University Press, 2001).
- Muhammad Zafulla Khan (New York: Olive Branch Press, 1997).
- N. J. Dawood (New York: Penguin Putnam, 1999).
- M. H. Shakir (Elmhurst, NY: Tahrike Tarsile Qur'ab, Inc., 2001).
- J. M. Rodwell (New York: Random House, 1993).
- A. J. Arberry (New York: Simon and Schuster, 1996).

FROM PEACE CHILD TO THE KORAN

Those who know my previous works—*Peace Child, Lords of the Earth* and *Eternity in Their Hearts*—will recall that I love to find and document a very fascinating feature of human cultures. I call it "redemptive analogy." Working as linguistic researchers, healers and educators among Stone Age tribes in West Papua, Indonesia, my wife, Carol, and I encountered native customs, legends and traditions that correspond, for example, with biblical accounts of Jesus' life and teaching. A sensitive advocate may use these fortuitous cultural elements as *bridges* to persuade endangered minority peoples to abandon such things as tribal war, headhunting and cannibalism—before the national police and their AK-47s make the choice for them *very* traumatically.

My Search for Redemptive Analogies

In *Peace Child*, I tell how Carol and I befriended a tribe of 3,000 cannibalistic headhunters—the Sawi. We found them living remotely in one of West Papua's vast swamps. We lived among them and learned their language. The Sawi were ravaged by malaria and other tropical diseases. Even more tragically, they were decimating their own population by waging almost constant warfare among themselves and with other tribes. As an alternative to that virtually genocidal violence, we urged the Sawi to find peace with God and with each other by believing the Christian message.

We hit a major barrier.

When I told the Sawi how Judas, one of Jesus' disciples, betrayed Jesus *with a kiss*, they exalted Judas as the hero of the story! They even bestowed upon him the title *taray duan* (a master of treachery)! One of the Sawi said, "We never thought of *kissing* victims of *our* treachery at the moment of truth. That Judas outdid us. He is the sort of fellow any other man should be proud to promise a daughter to in marriage."

My heart sank. I realized in that moment that treachery was the Sawi culture's "national pastime." What could I say to persuade them that Jesus was not a masterfully victimized dupe? How could I demonstrate that He, not Judas, was the hero?

As war raged on between two nearby Sawi villages, I repeatedly urged them to make peace, but saw little progress until Kaiyo, a father in one of the two villages, decided to honor my plea.

To make peace, Kaiyo made a sacrifice I could not imagine myself as a father ever being willing to make. He gave his son, Biakadon—his *only* child—to one of his enemies, a man named

Mahor. Deeply moved, Mahor embraced little Biakadon as a "peace child." He then invited every man, woman and child in the village of Kaiyo's enemies to lay a hand on little Biakadon, thereby pledging no violence against Kaiyo's village as long as his peace child remained alive in Mahor's house. I gasped in awe, realizing that long ago God had placed within the culture of the Sawi people something analogous to His redemptive provision for mankind through the sacrifice of His Son, Jesus Christ.

I began proclaiming Jesus as *the Tarop Tim Kodon* ("the ultimate Peace Child") given by *Navo Kodon (*"the ultimate Father, God, the Creator of everything").

This analogy proved to be more than just an eye-opener; it became a heart gripper. "If only you had told us that Judas's victim was a peace child," they assured me, "we would not have acclaimed Judas. To wrong a peace child is the most heinous crime possible." In faith, they began to *lay their hands* on Jesus, thereby pledging allegiance to God, the greatest peace-child giver of all. Headhunting ceased. Churches sprang up in every village. The Sawi learned to resolve misunderstandings through consultation rather than conflict.

Now they are healthier and happier, and their numbers are increasing.

Places of Refuge
Another tribe, the Yali—subjects of my second book, *Lords of the Earth*—had places of refuge. For them, Jesus became the *osowa ovelum* ("the perfect refuge"). In *Eternity in Their Hearts*, I record 25 more redemptive analogies from around the world. Not all of them are drawn from animistic cultures such as the Sawi and the Yali. For example, in China's 4,000-year-old pictographic script, a picture of a lamb above the first-person singular pronoun means "righteous." It actually reads "I under the lamb—righteous!" It serves as a kind of cultural compass pointing

Chinese people to Jesus, the righteousness-bestowing Passover lamb!

The Upside-Down Tree

To this day, almost everywhere I look I find more examples. An ancient text in India's *Vedas* describes a tree that is *upside down*, not because it has been uprooted, but because it is rooted in heaven with branches spreading above the earth, yielding fruit for mankind. The trunk of the upside-down tree, moreover, has been *gashed*, and the sap flowing from it like blood is for the healing of mankind.

ISLAM—THE GREAT EXCEPTION

Toward the end of our 15-year sojourn among the Sawi, Muslim immigrants from other more populous islands of Indonesia began bringing Islam to West Papua's tribes. Today Islam in Indonesia counts nearly 175 million followers.[1]

Gradually my attention shifted from the study of animistic cultures to the study of Islam. Eventually I traveled to various other Muslim nations: Malaysia, United Arab Emirates and Saudi Arabia. I have also encountered Muslims almost everywhere else I have gone. Then came September 11, 2001. As I watched and read coverage of Islamic terrorist attacks on the World Trade Center and the Pentagon, I knew what my next mission in life must be. I had to research my way into the roots of Islam itself, beginning with its founder and its foundations in the Koran.

Could I—finder of redemptive analogies in India, China and among West Papua's wild tribes—find parallels also in the Koran or in Islam's other sacred writings? As a Sawi redemptive analogy served to turn Sawi away from tribal war, could a Koranic redemptive analogy, clearly identified, serve to turn radical Muslims away from terrorism?

I had already gleaned considerable knowledge about the Muslim world before September 11. Now I had to *closely* examine Islam's own literary sources. I read multiple translations of the Koran. I also pored over Islam's other body of sacred writings called the hadiths and read a shelfful of books to survey the findings of researchers before me.

What I discovered shocked me.

I learned that Islam is unique among non-Christian religions. It stands alone as the only belief system that, due to its very design, *frustrates* anyone who seeks to use the redemptive-analogy approach. Here is what happens: While Mohammed claims the Old and New Testaments were from God, we find that 1,400 years ago the Islamic "prophet" quite drastically *redefined* fundamental tenets, including the very concept of God. For example,

- Judeo-Christianity's God *keeps* His promises. Conversely, quite frequently Islam's God abrogates (cancels) promises made earlier. He may even contradict his own commands, leaving everything he ever said open to question.
- A Christian speaks about Jesus who, by His death, atoned for the sin of the world, providing redemption. But Islamic teachings declare that Jesus did *not* die and rise again. The concept of God requiring an atonement as His legal basis for absolving the guilty is not simply poorly understood in Islam, it is totally denied!
- Muslim writings accuse Christians of worshiping three gods and teaching that God had intercourse with Mary, causing her to conceive Jesus.
- Islamic texts redefine Judeo-Christianity's heaven in a surprisingly shameful manner, as I explain later.

- Jesus' New Testament directive to *"give to Caesar what is Caesar's, and to God what is God's"* (Matthew 22:21) approves the separation of religion from civil government. Islam, by contrast, binds religion and the state together with iron chains.

The more digging I did into the Koran the more I realized when it comes to Islam the redemptive-analogy approach cannot work. Therefore, I had to look at the religion—its founder and its teachings—through a different lens, something antithetical to redemptive analogies.

I carefully considered the spectrum of possibilities ranging from a nonoffensive, politically correct generalization to a harsher full-scale refutation. Feeling somewhat like an attorney quizzing an uncooperative witness, I have opted to approach this inquiry through the lens of interrogation. It could also be called investigative journalism coupled with passionate fact-based commentary. Drawing primarily upon what Muslims esteem as their most reliable source—the Koran itself—I have sought the truth about the Koran and Mohammed. In this book I present what I firmly believe is an eye-opening and necessary case. You, the readers—Christian, Muslim and all others—are a de facto jury, weighing the evidence I present. And, of course, God is the ultimate judge of all things.

As you read, try to cast off any presumptions you may have about Islam, Mohammed and the Koran. Look at the Koranic words and the actions of Islam's founder as described in Islamic sources. Open your eyes to the secrets that lie within the Koran's Arabic text and the truth that history unveils. Ask what it means today, for Muslims and for the entire world.

Christian readers may be asking why I am not putting a greater emphasis on how God's love conquers all evil and injustice. Be assured that the underlying foundation of this book rests fully on my deepest belief that God loves everyone, including Muslims, and on my sincere hope that God's love will break through with a revelation of factual knowledge.

I use an aggressive, investigative, interpretive tone, not to attack anyone but to fully reveal, understand and underscore the facts. I do not want to unleash a vitriolic assault that could be misinterpreted as a personal affront by individual Muslims. The vast majority of Muslims are not bad people.

In fact, as I examine the Koran, Mohammed's life, Muslim teachings and the writings of certain apologists for Islam, I am not implying every Muslim agrees with or even understands the problems rooted at the core of Islam. Nor do I contend that every Muslim blanketly defends all of Mohammed's actions and teaching. Moreover, I know that many Muslims do not read the Koran or they only read it in Arabic, yet do not understand the language. Sadly, many guardians of Islam have either hidden or twisted much of what lies at the religion's heart and foundation. In fact, honest peace-loving Muslim readers will surely need to reexamine their own faith once they have the facts. This is a chilling reality; yet—if we are to know peace—it is one that must be faced in our post-September-11 age.

With this in mind, let's open our eyes and begin to examine the secrets of the Koran.

Note

1. "Islam Today." *PBS*. http://www.pbs.org/empires/islam/faithtoday.html (accessed August 9, 2002).

A BOOK OF PEACE?

Since September 11, 2001, the Koran (sometimes spelled Quran or Qur'an) has been a hot seller—not only in the Arabic world but also in Western nations. Why are Western readers suddenly so interested in a book that is the founding charter of the religion called Islam? Some Muslims (adherents of Islam) hope that this upsurge in sales in Western nations will result in more converts to their religion. In reality, many Western Koran buyers are simply bothered by nagging questions: What is it about this Koran that al-Qaeda and other up-in-arms Muslim revolutionaries think authorizes terrorism? Does the Koran in any way support their radicalism, or is it really, as some Muslims vociferously claim, a book of peace?

Western media commentators generally dismiss Islamic terrorists as fanatics who quote the Koran facetiously simply to legitimize anti-American and anti-Israeli political objectives. Not long after the attacks in New York and Washington, D.C., President George W. Bush declared that Osama bin Laden and his cohorts had "hijacked" a great religion for their own deranged private objectives.[1]

> ## President Bush declared that Osama bin Laden and his cohorts had "hijacked" a great religion.

At the same time, however, other media reporters informed us that members of Osama bin Laden's al-Qaeda do not just *read* the Koran, but they actually memorize large portions of it! Some, such as John Walker Lindh—an American citizen trained by the al-Qaeda—even memorize all 6,151 verses! Could it be that their intimate knowledge of the Koran is part of what inspires them to wage war? If al-Qaeda terrorists are exploiting the Koran only as a religious façade for primarily political goals, surely memorizing a few key verses would suffice.

The same media inconsistently report that Western embassies in Muslim nations issue frequent bulletins warning non-Muslims to shop and sightsee any day but *Friday*. This is not because Muslim shops are closed on Friday. Nor is it because Islam has strict rules against meandering on its day of rest. *Islam has no day of rest.* Why then? Friday is when Muslims gather in mosques (during early morning hours or, in the tropics, during siesta) to pray and hear sermons from the Koran. Western embassies know that Muslims emerging from mosques—if incensed by having heard a particularly vitriolic sermon from the Koran—may sometimes attack Westerners bodily. If the Koran teaches Muslims to coexist *peacefully* with non-Muslims—as so many voices assure us it does—Friday should be the *safest* day for a non-Muslim to encounter crowds of Muslims in the streets of Islamabad, Karachi or Jakarta.

ANTI-WESTERN AND ANTI-ISRAEL ONLY? OR ANTI-CHRISTIAN ALSO?

Attacks on America and suicide bombings in Israel are thoroughly reported, but other mounting evidences of radical Islamic rage rarely reach our television screens. On rare occasions, and never with comment, we see al-Qaeda trainees barging—AK-47s at the ready—into a large room where a *cross* is displayed on a wall. Obviously the trainees are practicing to kill Christians engaged in worship.

Does that perhaps signify hatred for *American* Christians, but not for Christians in other nations? I fear not! Radical Muslim gunmen on October 29, 2001, invaded a church service in Bahawalpur, Pakistan, killing 16 Pakistani Christian worshipers—not Americans—in cold blood. The Muslim government of Sudan is committing genocide upon Nubian Christians in the southern part of that nation. There are also dispatches from eastern Indonesia's Maluku Islands about Laskar Jihad—philosophical cousin of Osama bin Laden's al-Qaeda terrorist cult—using armed force to compel hundreds of Indonesian Catholics to convert to Islam or die.

What did terrified Indonesian Catholics have to do to convert to Islam? Both men *and* women had to be circumcised! Nonsterilized scissors served as instruments. Death was the only option for anyone who refused. Could they not feign conversion to Islam at the cost of a painful and humiliating mutilation and then revert to Catholicism? Of course they could, but under the same original threat of death!

Islam's Sharia law—rigorously applied by Laskar Jihad—has an embedded "catch-22." Reverters are tagged as apostates, and the penalty for apostasy under Sharia law is death.

Instances of anti-American, anti-Israeli and anti-Christian violence erupting in so many parts of the Muslim world are increasing exponentially. We really have no choice. We must stop evading the question we would rather not ask. Since virtually all of those who are perpetrating that violence claim loyalty to and inspiration from Mohammed's Koran, could it in fact be true that *part* of the Koran was indeed written to inspire violence—a modern form of which could be interpreted as a call to crash jet aircraft transporting hundreds of passengers into buildings occupied by thousands of people?

If it is *not* true, then we non-Muslims need to do more than send troops to places such as Afghanistan. We need to help moderate Muslims—who commend the Koran as a book that inspires peace—in their mission to persuade radical Muslims to cease their damnable misinterpretation of that peace-inspiring book!

Conversely, what if the Koran *does* advocate peace, yes, but only on terms laid down by Islam? What if, in fact, the Koran—on any other basis—calls for *war* against all non-Muslims? In that case, what we naively think professedly moderate Muslim apologists mean when they speak of peace in the Koran is not what they really mean! What they call "peace" is then only a carrot dangling from a stick. Non-Muslim societies then are donkeys that are expected to plod after an ever-receding "peace" carrot.

Moderate apologists for Islam within our borders *and* Muslim terrorists striking from outside then appear—perhaps unwittingly—as conspiring operatives in a good cop/bad cop stratagem.

Islam, in that scenario, is a hostile supremacist force seeking to grip Western civilization between opposite arms of a great

Islamic pincer. We are viewed as criminals to be squeezed until at last we confess "the truth" of Islam.

Every medium constantly acknowledges the goals of al-Qaeda-type Muslim terrorists as twofold: politically anti-American and anti-Israeli. We must awaken to the fact that their goals are much wider. Abundant evidence reveals their goals to be just as viciously anti-Christian as well. And since Christianity is bigger than Judaism and, yes, even bigger than America, it is definitely the major target in the crosshairs of radical Islam's long-range planning.

There is more! Radical Islam claims authorization from the Koran to oppose not only Jews and Christians but also everyone who does not accept Mohammed as a prophet, the Koran as divinely inspired, Islam as the ultimate religion and Jihad as every Muslim's sacred duty. Thus Hindus, Buddhists, Taoists, New Agers,

If radical Muslim views of the Koran are correct, there will always be Muslims answering the Koran's call to violence.

atheists, agnostics, materialists, secular humanists and even truly moderate Muslims also stand in radical Islam's OK-to-kill corral. There can hardly be a more important concern in today's world.

If radical Muslim views of the Koran are correct, there will always be Muslims answering the Koran's call to violence. John Q. Public in every nation must be informed beyond mere concern for damage control and political expediency. Some voices seem concerned only to help Islam save face in the wake of the tragedies perpetrated on September 11, 2001. Is not preventing the loss of future victims a far greater concern?

EXAMINING THE KORAN

The next few chapters, guided by eight different English translations of Islam's Koran, examine what all Muslims credit as *words* that God caused the angel Gabriel to dictate in Arabic through Mohammed—Islam's Arab founder—to various scribes in the early 600s. Later chapters trace how the Koran's teachings influenced relations between Muslims and non-Muslims during the 1,300 to 1,400 years since various recitations of the Koran were correlated into one book in the deserts of Arabia.

If Mohammed returned today, would he praise Osama bin Laden and al-Qaeda, or would he side with moderate Muslims?

Did Mohammed (sometimes spelled Mohammad, Muhammad, Muhammed or Mahomet) really intend to inspire peace and goodwill to all men, as taught in the New Testament, or something quite opposite? What do the Koran itself and its influence in history reveal? Are radical Muslims such as Osama bin Laden in fact taking seriously what most Muslims simply *ignore* or do not understand in the Koran? If Mohammed returned today, would he praise Osama bin Laden and al-Qaeda, or would he side with moderate Muslims?

The mere fact that more than 1 billion Muslims esteem the Koran as divinely inspired makes it an extremely important book. The Koran is second only to the Bible, honored by 1.6 billion people, for its potential to influence human affairs from a religious perspective.

Still, millions of Muslims credit the Koran with divine inspiration without actually perusing it (just as millions who call themselves Jews or Christians rarely read their own Tenach or Bible). A friend of mine asked an Iranian Muslim woman named Peri, "Have you ever read the Koran?" Peri replied, "Well, no, but everyone knows what's in it."

Do they?

Devotees who credit a book with something as important as divine inspiration—without *really* knowing its contents—leave themselves vulnerable to imposters. Unscrupulous teachers, misrepresenting what God requires in the revered but unread book, may induce sincere people to commit—in God's name—crimes they would otherwise abhor.

Conversely, if a revered book actually *does* make criminal demands in the name of God, should not its devotees bless themselves and the rest of mankind by canceling their devotion to it?

We must ask ourselves: Are we talking about a book of peace or Mohammed's *Mein Kampf*? The following quotes from the Koran and the summary of how they have influenced Muslim policy from the 600s until today are for both secular people and for those who are religious—Christians, Jews, Hindus, Buddhists and, yes, for Muslims, too. Muslims who, like Peri from Iran, think they know what is in the Koran but have not actually read it, owe it to themselves to be better informed. This is the serious quandary now faced by millions of sincere peace-loving Muslims.

Muslim apologists—some of whom may prefer that the world be left ignorant of certain parts of the Koran—will almost certainly accuse me of misquoting the Koran. I reply in advance: Anyone with a personal computer may easily confirm the accuracy of my quotations on their own computer screens. Simply call up a search engine—Google.com for example—and enter "Koran."

You can then choose any one of the several websites providing immediate access to every word of the Koran.

THE WAR VERSES

Readers will have heard apologists for the Koran acknowledge that, yes, there are war verses in the Koran, but *only a few*. Every Muslim apologist hastens to add that the Koran's sparse number of war verses relate to just a few unavoidable military crises in Islam's early history. They assure us that no war verse was ever intended to serve as a model inciting Muslims in general to hostility against resistant non-Muslims in all ages.

What is the truth of the matter?

In fact, there are at least 109 identifiable *war verses* in the Koran. One out of every 55 verses in the Koran is a war verse. War verses are scattered throughout Mohammed's chapters like blood splatter at a crime scene. I will demonstrate from Mohammed's own words that he leaves readers in no doubt—he obviously intended his war verses to arouse Muslims to compel the conversion of non-Muslims to Islam, even by violence if necessary. Failing their conversion, Mohammed ordained that non-Muslims be killed, enslaved or—provided Islam is in full political control—heavily taxed for the advancement of Islam in perpetuity!

And yet I hesitate. Why? If I simply cite war verse after war verse after war verse from among 109 samples, many readers, seeing just the words on paper, may think it was just that—vengeful-sounding *words* that got written on paper but remain innocent because they did not lead to actual *deeds* of violence. Even Hitler's *Mein Kampf*—minus World War II—could be justified by some as Adolph's way of venting frustration. Thus I am obligated to quote Mohammed's war verses in the context of the actual violence they either described or inspired. Violent words that trigger violent deeds cannot be dismissed as *innocent ramblings*.

The tragic events I describe in the next few pages are all confirmed *from Muslim sources*. Readers may find it odd that perpetrators of such loathsome crimes would confess them so audaciously. In fact, the violence that Mohammed inspired in his followers was so pervasive that both he and they seem to have lost all sense of how villainous the recounting of their deeds would appear to non-Muslim readers in ages to come. As the following chapter shows, they virtually *brag* about murdering innocents.

Note

1. Steven Waldman, "A Great Moment for Muslims," *beliefnet*, www.beliefnet.com/story/90/story_9015.html (accessed July 29, 2002).

THE WOLF IN THE FOLD

To understand the secrets of the Koran we must begin by learning something of the life of the man who, according to Islamic history, originated it. His name was Mohammed.

The most commonly accepted year for Mohammed's birth is A.D. 571. He was born in Mecca (sometimes spelled Makkah), a major center on a north-south caravan route roughly paralleling the Red Sea in western Arabia. Mecca also guarded the Ka'aba—a shrine sheltering 360 idols representing the 360 gods that various pagan Arab tribes worshiped.

Orphaned in childhood and raised by an uncle, Mohammed never became literate. Still, he worked his way up to managerial status in a Meccan caravan company owned by a wealthy widow, Khadija. He and Khadija married. Khadija was several years Mohammed's senior, yet she bore him four daughters.

Early in the 600s, Mohammed began to follow the ways of Arab seers seeking spiritual enlightenment. He resorted to a cave on Mount Hira, near Mecca. Soon he claimed to be experiencing visitations from Gabriel, an archangel mentioned by Jews and Christians. Gabriel, he said, appeared to him on behalf of the same God that Jews and Christians worshiped. Mohammed called that God Allah.

This entity identified as Gabriel began explaining what Mohammed must do as a servant for Allah. He had to oppose the idolatrous worship of pagan idols wherever they were found—especially the idols in Mecca's Ka'aba. Much to the displeasure of wealthy keepers of the Ka'aba, Mohammed proclaimed himself a prophet and began preaching vehemently against pagan idolatry. Eventually, in A.D. 622, Meccan hostility to his ardent monotheism forced Mohammed to flee with a few followers to Medina, another caravan stop located some 200 miles north of Mecca.

The few Meccans who fled with Mohammed were those who readily accepted, at face value, his claim that the God of the Jews and Christians had appointed him as a prophet for Arabs. Some Arabs who disbelieved Mohammed's message did so because they quite frankly preferred to worship idols. Others simply demurred, saying in effect, "You claim to be a prophet like the prophets Jews and Christians believe in, but we Arabs have never had prophets like that, so we don't know how to determine who is or isn't [sent by God] to be that kind of a prophet. . . . But Jews know how to recognize that kind of a prophet. So if they confirm your claim, we will believe you. Otherwise, we retain our own beliefs."[1]

Wanting to win followers in Medina faster than was possible in Mecca, the center of Arabian idolatry, Mohammed found himself burdened with an urgent public relations need to have Jews affirm his claim to biblical prophethood.

The relatively few Jews who resided in Mecca—less literate than their better-read compatriots in Medina—apparently preferred to leave judgment regarding Mohammed's claims to the latter. Jews in Mecca—a tiny minority in that city—understandably preferred not to become embroiled in the festering "Mohammed problem."

Jews in Medina, however—much to their later regret, no doubt—did find themselves increasingly pressured by curious Arabs in Medina to voice their opinions regarding the so-called prophet from Mecca.

THE PROBLEM OF FINDING SUPPORT FOR MOHAMMED'S CLAIMS

In Medina, Mohammed offered his services to the city as an arbiter of disputes. In that role, he constantly sought to ingratiate himself with fellow Arabs and, at first, with the city's sizable Jewish population.

Mohammed could not offer a single physical miracle as evidence of prophethood.

Watching him arbitrate disputes, the Jews also observed Mohammed closely, looking for any signs that he had received prophetic gifting from God. The ability to work miracles would have been one proof, but Mohammed could not offer a single physical miracle as evidence of prophethood. In fact, passages in the Koran express his dismay over people who kept demanding miracles as support for his claims. Sans miracles, what else could Mohammed offer?

Demonstrating prowess in offering revelations confirming the Old Testament was very likely Mohammed's only other way of impressing Medinan Jews. However, the Koran itself shows that his knowledge of the Jewish sacred books was shockingly deficient. Even what he claimed to be divine inspiration could not compensate for Mohammed's personal lack of knowledge of Scripture.

A Glaring Omission

If the first 89 chapters of the Koran, compiled years later, offer any clues to the content of Mohammed's early revelations, he probably treated the Jews in Medina to a narration he surely felt would spellbind them: the Exodus story! The Koran would later feature Mohammed's renditions of Moses' confrontation with the pharaoh, a ruler of ancient Egypt, 27 times in his first 89 chapters. In other words, Mohammed repeated that same story once every 3.3 chapters! It surely must have been one of his favorite pulpit pieces.

Alas, not even *once* in 27 tellings of the Exodus saga did Mohammed include *the* most integral component of the story: *the Passover!* How could the Jews accept as a prophet a man who— if he even knew about the Passover—had no sense of its importance?

More Gaps in Mohammed's Knowledge

Omitting the Passover from the Exodus story was not Mohammed's only lapse. The Koran would later reveal that he thought Adam and Eve sinned, not in an earthly garden, but in paradise. Mohammed had the erring couple cast to Earth only *after* they sinned (see Koran 7:19-24 or 7:20-25). Some Muslim translators

M. Z. Khan translated the Koran with English rather than Arabic forms for the names of biblical characters, yet strangely replaces Saul with its Arabic spelling, Talut. Why? To hide Mohammed's error from non-Arab speakers? M. M. Ali, another Muslim writer, argues that there were two different parties of 300 men each. His basis: Gideon's men camped near a spring; Saul's army drank from a river. But Judges 6:33 reveals that the Jordan River was *nearby*. Would Gideon have waited upon 10,000 men to drink from a mere spring or from a river?

try to veil his error by using the word "garden" instead of "paradise," yet even they let the truth out a few verses later, when God, *after* the test, said to Adam and Eve, **"Get you down . . . earth will for a while provide your dwelling" (Koran 7:24).**

Mohammed further taught that Haman, a Persian in the Bible's book of Esther, was an associate of the pharaoh in Egypt 900 years earlier in the days of Moses (see Koran 28:5-6,8). Of course to accept this Muslims must assume that a Persian name, Haman, was coincidentally also a male name in Egypt centuries earlier.

Mohammed also confused King Saul—mentioned in the Old Testament book of 1 Samuel—with Gideon who, in Judges 7:1-7, chose 300 warriors out of 10,000 men by observing how they drank water (see Koran 2:249 or 250).

A Whimsical Legend Canonized

Somewhere Mohammed heard a curious Jewish legend. Whoever concocted it claimed that when God gave the Law to Israel at Mount Sinai, Israel initially refused to promise to receive it. How did God compel them to obey and open their eyes? He lifted the entire mass of Mount Sinai up from Earth and held it in the sky above the camp of Israel. Thinking God was about to drop the mountain on their heads, Israel quickly relented!

How startled Medinan Jews must have been to find Mohammed treating one of their legends as a valid part of Old Testament Scripture.[2] How could Mohammed expect Jews to accept his "revelations," riddled with these and numerous similar outright errors, as confirming the Old Testament? More to the point: How could he continue offering erroneous renditions of Old Testament stories in a city where literate Jews would be forever correcting his errors—probably even guffawing over them publicly?[3]

How did Mohammed respond to Jewish ridicule? He had three options: confess he was not a prophet, relocate to a city with no Jews or *purge all resistant Jews* from Medina. To his shame, Mohammed presaged the catastrophic choice another world leader would make centuries later—he chose to *purge the Jews*.

Troops of modern Muslim apologists, whitewash and brush in hand, strain their brains trying to justify the original minigenocide that Mohammed was about to unleash upon the Jews in Medina. They also try to disconnect his murders there from the numerous copycat atrocities that his followers, honoring his example, were to perpetrate down through the subsequent centuries of Islamic history.

I call them modern Muslim apologists because during most of the 1,400 years since Mohammed's time Muslims have enjoyed such total control in North Africa and the Middle East that few people ever dared ask them to justify anything. Times are different now, and Muslims are trying to develop apologetic skills. But they have yet to encounter the full weight of critical investigation of which free Western minds are capable. In other words, the ground has just begun to heat up under Islam's feet.

Some apologists label the horrors that were about to occur in Medina as a just defensive war against the Jews. Could it have been that? Repeatedly in the Koran, Mohammed criticizes some Jews for dismissing his claims, others for selling bits of their Scriptures **"for a paltry price" (Koran 2:41)** or for hiding Scripture from Arabs. Yet nowhere in the Koran does Mohammed accuse the Jews of a single act of physical aggression against him. In fact, a larger collection of Islamic literature—the hadiths—discloses that Jews in Medina taunted, criticized or opposed Mohammed and his followers on intellectual grounds, but there is no mention of any Jew threatening physical action.

Some apologists label the horrors in Medina as a just defensive war against the Jews.

Arabs in Medina were asking Jews for their honest evaluation of Mohammed. Medinan Jews were freely offering their opinions. Little did they know that exercising the freedom of speech they had always enjoyed prior to Mohammed's arrival would seal the doom of many among them.

Still, before Mohammed could retaliate against Medinan Jews for causing him to lose face, he had to win the collusion of Medinan pagans, a majority of whom respected the Jews. To lull suspicion and buy time for plotting, Mohammed and the relatively few followers he had led from Mecca ratified a seemingly benign treaty with both pagans and Jews in Medina. It was called the Constitution of Medina. It granted to Mohammed the sole right to arbitrate disputes. It also bound all parties involved—Muslims, pagans and Jews—to peaceful coexistence.

Every rational person knew that someone—a Muslim, a pagan or a Jew—by accident, carelessness, human folly, drunkenness or in a fit of temper, would eventually do something that violated the treaty. When a breach finally happened, everyone would expect Mohammed, the arbiter, to step in, adjudicate the wrong and preserve the peace. Little did anyone guess that Mohammed would bide his time, awaiting the day when *a Jew* would finally be found guilty of abusing the treaty. When that fateful day came, Mohammed would suddenly show no interest in arbitration. Instead, he would immediately declare the constitution horribly violated and exploit the offense of one Jewish person as a *cassus belli* against an entire community of Jews. Thus his appointment as de facto keeper of the constitution—a seemingly benign pact—would actually afford Mohammed leverage at a later time to avenge himself upon the Jews with an appearance of legality.

The fact that Medinan Jews signed the treaty confirms their willingness, at least at that stage, to trust Mohammed as an arbiter, if not as a prophet. They may even have hoped that keeping him occupied in politics might be good for *him*. Stir up a little political ambition, and maybe it would distract him from his other career, the one the Jews knew he was *not* cut out for: biblical prophethood.

But Mohammed was not about to devote more than a small portion of time to Medinan politics. Denied the public-relations advantage that Jewish endorsement for his claims would have brought—Mohammed turned to other enticements he was sure many pagan Arabs would relish: military prowess, plunder and *sex*.

Taking their swords, Mohammed and his band began venturing out from Medina as a base. They marauded caravans traveling between Mecca and Syria. For author Ibn Warraq, a former Muslim, Mohammed during this period was "no more than the head of a robber community, unwilling to earn an honest living."[4]

Was Mohammed merely an Arabian Jesse James? Or was he something far more sinister? As quotes in the next chapter show, Mohammed distributed *women and girls* he captured on raids to be sex slaves for his male followers. He kept some for himself, of course.[5] Otherwise reticent pagan men were thus enticed to become Muslims.

Of course some of Mohammed's male followers would complain that if they were killed while marauding, they would not get to enjoy the promised extra sex. Unabashed, Mohammed was ready with a shameless retort that is still taken seriously by hundreds of millions of credulous Muslim men, even in today's world.

In the Koran, he repeatedly redefines Judeo-Christianity's *heaven* as an enormous God-owned bordello in the sky. In that heavenly brothel, loyal Muslim men—especially those paying the door price of martyrdom—would find a host of virgins, called *houris*, who would forever satisfy all their sexual cravings (see Koran 38:51; 44:54; 55:55-74; 56:22,34-36). In fact, sex with beautiful houris in heaven was guaranteed to be far more enjoyable than any sex Muslim men might miss by being killed while serving God or by trying to have promiscuous sex here on Earth.

If a follower complained sardonically that early martyrs would get to deflower all the virginal houris, leaving later Muslim martyrs with used goods, Mohammed had an answer for that as well. Rodwell's translation describes the houris as **"a rare creation . . . we have made them ever virgins" (Koran 56:34-36)**. Ahmed Ali translates "God's" description of the houris in the same passage: **"Maidens incomparable. We have formed them in a distinctive fashion, and made them virginal."**

Muslim scholars tend to find a deeper meaning behind these words. One interpretation: heavenly houris are a rare, incomparable and distinctive kind of virgin precisely because, once deflowered, they become physically virginal again for the next sex act.

This gave Jews and any Christians living in Medina even more cause to feel appalled at Mohammed's claim to biblical prophethood. For a male in Judaism, marrying one wife is the ideal. The idea of promiscuous sex, in this life or beyond, is abhorrent. As a guide for Christians, Jesus taught that people welcomed into God's holy presence *"will neither marry nor be given in marriage; they will be like the angels in heaven"* (Mark 12:25).

Mohammed repeatedly redefines Judeo-Christianity's *heaven* as an enormous God-owned bordello in the sky.

What happens to a married couple's sense of the sanctity of their marriage if thoughts of future sex with houris keeps distracting the husband from cherishing his wife and the wife from enjoying her husband because she knows he's thinking about them? For anyone who takes the Koran seriously, there is probably nothing more corrosive to true marital bliss than this bit of mischief.

Interestingly, I have not found anything in either the Koran or the hadiths that denotes *angels* as sexual beings. Yet *fallen angels*, i.e., demons (called *jinn* in Arabic), are clearly described as capable of having sex with houris. For example, Ahmed Ali's translation of the Koran describes houris as **"undeflowered by man or by jinn" (55:74)**.

How strange that Mohammed leaves Muslim men in heaven *below* the more exalted angelic state. Instead of blissfully worshiping God, casting their crowns at His feet, apparently Muslim men must spend eternity doing exactly what demons would do if given a chance: couple with one houri after another forever.

Ruthless enticement of the male sex drive, combined with the prospect of bountiful earthly plunder, soon brought a majority of Medina's pagan men to Mohammed's side. Indeed, the allurement of Mohammed's promise of eternal sensuous pleasure in paradise could have a strange effect on male followers. Historian Maxime Rodinson recounts that an Arab man named Umayr Ibn al-Humam, hearing Mohammed promise immediate access to paradise for anyone martyred in battle raging at the time, shouted:

> "Fine! Fine! Have I only to get myself killed by these men to enter into paradise?" . . . Grasping his sword, [he] plunged into the thick of the battle and was soon killed.[6]

Umayr Ibn al-Humam was perhaps the first among uncounted thousands of death-courting Muslim martyrs who over centuries—and still today—mislay their faith on Mohammed's pernicious fantasy. Thus do they waste the precious gift of life—their own and others'—even in suicide bombings.

LONG-TERM SIDE EFFECTS OF MOHAMMED'S USE OF THE SEX LURE

Islam's strong cultural preference is to keep Muslim women and girls so completely covered that virtually nothing of their femininity is evident when they venture outdoors. In Saudi Arabia even a woman's face and eyes must be veiled. *Newsweek* gave the world a shocking example of how rigid this obsession can be. For the full report, see *Newsweek* (July 22, 2002). Here is my summary:

> In Mecca, a fire broke out in an intermediate school housing 750 Muslim girls. Every window was covered with iron bars to assure that no male prowler or lovesick boyfriend

could ever steal in. Every door was locked. As girls rushed down a flight of stairs toward the only door that was used for exit/reentry, 15 were trampled to death and some 40 others injured. Alas, the one door was locked. The Muslim religious policeman who was supposed to be on duty to unlock the door in an emergency was off on an errand.

Finally, someone managed to open the door and hundreds of terrified girls rushed into the street to escape the suffocating smoke and encroaching flame. In their hurry to escape, however, they did not have time to go to their rooms to get the obligatory head coverings they needed to venture out-of-doors. A score of Muslim religious policemen (called *Mutawas*), outraged at seeing bare-headed girls swarming openly in a public street, converged on the scene with one intent—to guard the decency of the community *by forcing the girls back into the burning building!*

Thankfully the civic police had more sense. But they had to beat some of the Mutawas senseless to keep them from pursuing their fanatic goal of pushing girls back into the burning building *just because males in the street might see their uncovered faces.*[7]

Granting that some other cultures allow excessive public exposure of the female form, something at Islam's beginning stimulated core Islam to its strong insistence on *total* covering. What could that have been?

Consider what must have been the social effect of Mohammed's constant bandying of the promise of increased sex with extra wives and female slaves in this life plus even more and better eternal sex with bevies of virgins in paradise. Understandably, pagan Arab men, snagged into Islam by this almost irresistible lure of sex, had sex on their minds even more than before their "conversions."

This presented a dilemma. No Muslim man wanted *his own* wives and daughters to become objects of so much increased male sexual desire in the general community. So Muslim men felt obliged to cover and even hide their wives and daughters from view even more than pagan Arab culture originally required. What began as a practical safeguard soon became an entrenched cultural imperative.

The Problem of Female Genital Mutilation

Islam's widespread practice of amputating the clitoris and sometimes part or even all of the vulva from the genitalia of Muslim women, affirmed in a *hadith* by Mohammed himself, most likely also traces back to the founder's deliberate abuse of sex to lure pagan males into his cult.[8] The more the male sex drive is purposefully aroused, the more the female sex urge may have to be proportionately suppressed, lest orgiastic hell begin to spread.

Consider then what frequently happens when even a modestly clothed young Western woman walks alone in broad daylight down a street in, for example, a non-Westernized area of a city in Pakistan. Muslim men around her can see her face, hair and neck—maybe even her ankles. Some of them perceive that much exposure as intent on her part to arouse them. The fact that she is not accompanied by a male relative confirms their suspicions. Knowing that she, a Western woman, has not been subjected to that cruel amputation which Islam forces upon millions of Muslim women, some males may even imagine that she must feel sexual desire for *them*.

They tend also to perceive themselves as not responsible to exercise decent social restraint. Rather *she* is responsible not to tempt them! Whatever lewd thing Muslim men around her say, do or feel as a result is regarded as her fault alone.

Little wonder that thousands of Western women in such situations have complained of being groped, leered at and insulted.

In major cities of Malaysia and Indonesia, where cultures mix, such problems are less likely, but if *rioting* breaks out in Indonesia, the world's most populous predominantly Muslim nation, *anything* can happen, even in a major city.

During a major upheaval in Indonesia in the late 1990s, sex-crazed Muslim men gang-raped dozens of Chinese women in shops, homes and even in the streets, shouting in Arabic, *"Allahu Akbar!"* (God is great!).[9]

Author Jan Goodwin's *Price of Honor* exceeds even Betty Mahmoody's *Not Without My Daughter* in documenting the horrors that women frequently experience in the Middle East. Goodwin records hundreds of instances of Muslim women beaten into submission, harassed in their homes and even subjected to *public* molestation. For example:

> Working women in Cairo have long complained of being sexually assaulted on buses by men who take the opportunity of rare proximity to the opposite sex to knead, rub and fondle female commuters. . . . Since being manhandled is so shameful [to report] decent women suffer in silence rather than be accused of having encouraged the man.[10]

Goodwin then writes of Shahinaz, a young woman *raped* on a bus in Egypt: "Fundamentalists began saying it was the girl's fault. She was wearing a skirt . . . not a *hijab*. The media also began to blame her. . . . Even women said it was her fault . . . she was working, not staying at home."[11] Still, Goodwin lacks the awesomely needed courage to lay the blame for such horrors right where it belongs—*on Mohammed, the Koran and Islam*. Millions of modern media people are like doctors describing horrible symptoms but failing to identify the virus.

Consider another symptom traceable to the same virus: The *Los Angeles Times*, July 4, 2002, on page A4, reported a strange example of the perception of justice in a Muslim tribal area of Pakistan. I summarize: A male youth was seen walking beside a girl from another tribe. A local tribal council ruled that this outrage had to be punished, but no one handed the young man over to Pakistan's civic police to be punished by civil law. No, this "crime" was deemed an offense against Muslim Sharia law and against the dignity of those offended. A local council of elders decided to punish the young man by decreeing that his 18-year-old sister be gang-raped. Apparently the sentence was carried out. Pakistan's civic police reportedly were seeking to arrest the rapists. There seemed to be no mention of arresting the elders who decreed the *boy's* punishment.

In later chapters I explain more of the dire effect Mohammed's teachings have had upon women. Now back to Mohammed's buildup for a day of vengeance against Jews in Mecca.

THE BATTLE OF BADR

The larger Mohammed's force became in Medina, the bolder he grew in shattering the previously existing peace by raiding caravans moving to or from Mecca. One day Mohammed, en route to raid a caravan, was intercepted by an armed force from Mecca near a well called Badr.

Mohammed's 330 fighters defeated the larger Meccan force, killing 49 men. Sir William Muir and Rodinson opine that the Meccans, recognizing some of their own clansmen in Mohammed's contingent, lost the battle because they did not have the heart to kill relatives.[12] Mohammed, on the other hand, constantly taught his followers that loyalty to Islam overrode all other human bonds (see Koran 9:23-24; 58:22-23). Thus his men did not hesitate in battle, even when swinging the sword at Meccans whom they recognized as relatives.

An omen of deepening moral darkness fell that day. Someone cast the severed head of a slain Meccan at Mohammed's feet. Ibn Warraq describes Mohammed's response: "It [the severed head] is more acceptable to me than the choicest camel in all Arabia."[13]

Researchers overwhelmingly agree: Mohammed's victory at Badr enhanced his ability to believe (some imply to feign belief) in his own claim to prophethood. It also encouraged him to think that his plan to wage war against the sizable number of Jews in Medina was closer to fulfillment.

Having shattered the peace between Mecca and Medina, Mohammed next set out to destroy the commendable concord that Arabs and Jews in Medina had enjoyed for centuries.

The wolf was in the fold.

Mohammed knew he could not attack Medina's Jews without the complicity of Arabs who had long lived as their neighbors. Riding a wave of heightened prestige after his victory at Badr, he still needed a way to test if he could murder Jews without triggering a reaction of horror among Medinan Arabs. Arab public conscience, though pagan, was still too moral to be Mohammed's ally. It was an enemy he had to degrade.

Mohammed found a way to keep measuring how much mind control he had achieved among Medinan pagan Arabs. After the Battle of Badr, he began ordering a series of heinous assassinations of individual Arabs. If Arabs could bear to see a few of their own people slain for offending him, surely they were not far from consenting to the wholesale slaughter of *Jews* for the same reason.

The self-proclaimed prophet's first victim was a hapless Meccan named al-Nader—killed because "he had scoffed at Mohammed . . . and told better stories than the prophet himself."[14]

His next prey was Ocba, a captive taken at Badr. Ocba, about to be slain, asked:

> "And my little girl. Who will take care of her?"
>
> "Hellfire!" exclaimed the Prophet; and on the instant the victim was hewn to the ground. "Wretch that thou wast!" [Mohammed] continued, "and persecutor! Unbeliever in God, in his Prophet, and in his Book!"[15]

Al-Nader and Ocba were Arabs—from Mecca, not Medina. To see if he could order an actual citizen of *Medina* slain without triggering repercussions, Mohammed turned with lethal malice, not to condemn a man, but a woman.

An Arab poetess named Asma bint Marwan wrote couplets chiding Arab men of Medina for gathering like seduced women around the treacherous stranger from Mecca. She likened them to "men greedy for meal soup when it is cooking,"[16] perhaps referring to their hope of gaining plunder and sex slaves via Mohammed's continuing raids. When her poem was read to him,

> Muhammed said aloud, "Will no one rid me of this daughter of Marwan?" There was a man present who belonged to the poetess's clan . . . Umayr ibn Adi . . . that very evening he went to the poetess's house. She was sleeping with her children about her. The youngest, still at the breast, lay asleep in her arms. [Umayr] drove his sword through her, and in the morning he went to Muhammad. "Messenger of God," he said, "I have killed her!"
>
> "You have done a service to Allah and his Messenger, Umayr," was the reply.[17]

Rodinson's and Warraq's sources have the murderer asking if he should fear retaliation. Mohammed, apparently knowing that Asma's outnumbered clan could not risk a blood feud, assured Umayr that not even two goats would bother to butt heads over Asma's murder.[18]

Outnumbered and apparently terrorized into abject submission, Asma's entire clan, Banu Khatma, converted to Islam. In the history of Islam, Muslim teachers tend to interpret such a result as justifying the crime that led to it. This is one of radical Islam's rationalizations for terrorism—slaughter a few; reap the conversion of many.

> **Mohammed, who had served Medina as an arbitrator, decided to drop the "arbi" and become just a traitor.**

One month after Asma was murdered, another of Mohammed's accomplices killed another Arab poet who had dared to criticize Mohammed: 100-year-old Abu Afak.[19]

The indefensible absence of Arab public protest to these outrages persuaded Mohammed that he could at last begin to move against Medinan Jews. Their knowledge-based criticisms stung him far more gallingly than intuition-based barbs from Arab poets. As keeper of the constitution mentioned earlier, Mohammed needed a default on the part of the Jews—a default he could use to justify retaliation.

A foolish Jewish goldsmith of the Banu Qaynuqa clan gave Mohammed exactly the excuse he needed. The goldsmith publicly embarrassed the wife of a Muslim. Another Muslim overreacted by killing the goldsmith. The Jews killed the Muslim who killed the goldsmith. What would arbiter Mohammed do to restore the peace?

Nothing.

The man who until then had served Medina as an arbitrator decided to drop the "arbi" and become just a traitor. In violation of his appointed duty, he in effect declared the Constitution of Medina no longer valid and attacked the Banu Qaynuqa Jews.

Why didn't the arbitrator *arbitrate* instead of *laying siege*?

Scores of Muslim apologists—and some naive non-Muslim scholars who take Muslim scholars' word on almost anything—claim that Medinan Jews were guilty of aggression against Mohammed and justly needed to be opposed. But they supply no examples—beyond the Jews' very justifiable intellectual confrontation.

Some scholars claim that Jews were about to attack Muslims physically. Shouting in denial stand two striking facts: First is that Medina's other two Jewish clans did not rush to take sides with the one that Mohammed chose to attack. Common sense would have dictated opposing him *in unison* if in fact it was their plan to physically oppose him at all.

Second, when an army from Mecca responded to Mohammed's caravan raiding and to the loss at Badr by attacking Medina itself, several thousand Jews uprising within the city would have given Mecca the victory. That occasion—called the Battle of the Ditch—was a day of golden opportunity for the Jews if in fact they were plotting against Mohammed. Why did they not exploit it? Clearly they had no military plan. They were merchants who wanted peace.

Fifteen days later, cut off from supplies of food, the Banu Qaynuqa surrendered. Mohammed planned to slay every Jewish male, but a sufficient number of Medinan Arabs objected to so utterly cruel a plan. So Mohammed settled for evicting all Banu Qaynuqa families from their homes, even from their own hometown.

With only what they could carry, Qaynuqa Jews fled on camel or on foot toward Christian Syria. Muslim despoilers looted the goods that remained and claimed all Banu Qaynuqa homes and land. Mohammed himself took one-fifth of everything.[20]

Next to die by assassination was another poet, Kab ibn al-Ashraf.[21] Mohammed then ordered, "Kill any Jew you are able to kill."[22] Muhayyisa, a Muslim, responded by killing a Jew named Ibn Sunayna.

Victory over the Banu Qaynuqa brought Mohammed to a second phase of his plot to extinguish Jewish freedom of thought and speech in Medina. He attacked, defeated and banished the wealthy Nadir. Their riches, houses and lands made Mohammed even *more* financially secure. Two years later and in another location Mohammed massacred the Nadir anyway.

Finally, Mohammed besieged the last major Jewish tribe in Medina, the Banu Qurayza. Warned that Mohammed *this time* wanted blood, not banishment, the Jews offered to surrender on condition that their fate be decided by the one group of Medinan Arabs that Mohammed had not yet totally seduced—the Banu Aws. At worst, the Jews must have thought they would be banished from their homes, as were the two other Jewish clans.

It was not to be.

How the Banu Qurayza must have regretted that they and the second clan expelled had not sided with the Banu Qaynuqa when Mohammed launched his first attack. Apparently there was no Winston Churchill-like leader to warn the three Jewish clans: "If we do not hang together, we will each hang separately."

Refusing the Banu Aws as mediators, Mohammed feigned compromise by appointing Sa'd, an Arab who was secretly Mohammed's accomplice, to decide the fate of the third Jewish clan. Sa'd waited until all the Banu Qurayza men gave up their weapons. Then, as Sa'd knew Mohammed required, he ordered every Jewish man beheaded.

Multiple unabashed Muslim sources varyingly describe Mohammed himself presiding over the beheading of at least 500 Jewish men, five at a time.[23] Their bodies were buried in a long ditch. Other Muslim sources place the number of Jewish men slain as high as 900. Their wives and daughters became sex slaves for Muslim men. Jewish boys not needed for labor (or old enough to perhaps desire later to avenge the fate of their parents) were sold for profit. Mohammed seized Rayhana, widow of one of the Jews he had slain, and forced her to be one of his concubines.[24] Thus did Mohammed validate the Jews' refusal to accept him as a prophet—then and forever!

These are just a few of the violent *deeds* that form the context of 109 war verses in the Koran. Historian Bat Ye'or asserts: "During his Medina period, Mohammed undertook no less than thirty-eight raids."[25]

Notes

1. Maxime Rodinson, *Muhammad* (New York: Pantheon Books, 1971), p 161.
2. I can only wonder if Mohammed's subsequent advocacy of *the use of force* to compel conversion to Islam, Koran 2:257 notwithstanding, can be traced back to his mistaking this peculiar legend for an accurate description of divine behavior.
3. Rodinson, *Muhammad*, p. 185.
4. Ibn Warraq, *Why I Am Not a Muslim* (Amherst, NY: Prometheus Books, 1995), p. 92.
5. Rodinson, *Muhammad*, p. 196; Warraq, *Why I Am Not a Muslim*, p. 96.
6. Rodinson, *Muhammad*, p. 167.
7. Paraphrased from *Newsweek* (July 22, 2002), n.p.
8. Jean Sasson, *Daughters of Arabia* (London: Bantam Books, 1994), p. 207.
9. "Chinese Woman Forced to Watch Gang Rape and Burning Death of Her Sisters," June 1998, *colorq*, http://www.colorq.org/humanrights/indonesia/Jakarta.htm (accessed August 25, 2002).
10. Jan Goodwin, *Price of Honor: Muslim Women Lift the Veil of Silence on the Islamic World* (London: Warner Books, 1998), p. 339.
11. Ibid.
12. Rodinson, *Muhammad*, p. 167.
13. Warraq, *Why I Am Not a Muslim*, p. 93.

14. Ibid.
15. Ibid.
16. Ibid.
17. Ibid., p. 94.
18. Rodinson, *Muhammad*, p. 174; Warraq, *Why I Am Not a Muslim*, p. 94.
19. Warraq, *Why I Am Not a Muslim*, p. 94.
20. Rodinson, *Muhammad*, p. 174; Warraq, *Why I Am Not a Muslim*, p. 94.
21. Warraq, *Why I Am Not a Muslim*, p. 94.
22. Ibid., p. 95.
23. Rodinson, *Muhammad*, p. 213; Warraq, *Why I Am Not a Muslim*, p. 96.
24. Rodinson, *Muhammad*, p. 213.
25. Bat Ye'or, *Islam and Dhimmitude: Where Civilizations Collide* (Cranbury, NJ: Associated University Presses, 2002), pp. 36-37.

CHAPTER THREE

VIOLENT VERSES, VIOLENT DEEDS

As Mohammed ratcheted the levels of violence upward, he audaciously kept naming God as his accomplice.

> **You were encamped on this** [the near] **side of the valley ... with the caravan below ... you would have surely declined [to fight]; but God sought to accomplish what he had ordained (Koran 8:43;** see also 8:42**).**

Muslim apologists insist that Mohammed urged his followers to perpetrate violence only in *self-defense* (which in the
Muslim view includes retaliation). That claim is false. Muslim
aggression against non-Muslims (called infidels) is authorized
in dozens of verses. All anyone needed to do to be named an infidel—prompting Mohammed to cry "War!"—was to refuse to
acknowledge that Mohammed was a prophet or that his Koran
was inspired by God.

Verses in which Mohammed promoted violence as justified
for self-defense are far fewer in number, but there are several:

**Believers! Retaliation is decreed for you in blood-
shed (2:178).**

**Fight for the sake of God those who fight against
you, but do not attack them first . . . slay them wherever you find them. Drive them out of the places
from which they drove you (2:190-191).**

There is no evidence that the three Jewish clans Mohammed
purged from Medina ever drove Muslims from their homes or
physically assaulted them. In fact, some Jews even fought alongside Muslims to defend Medina in the Battle of the Ditch. How
easily Islam's prophet could forget his own stipulation to fight
only in self-defense.

Mohammed continued:

**Fight against them until idolatry is no more and
God's religion reigns supreme. But if they desist,
fight none except the evil-doers (Koran 2:193; 8:39).**

What begins as retaliation ends with Islam enthroned as the
only religion and the Muslim God as the only one worthy of

worship. Amazingly, M. M. Ali apparently wants us to think that Mohammed, in the above quote, actually advocates total freedom of religion! Ali writes:

> When persecution ceases and men are not forced to accept or renounce a religion, being at liberty to profess any religion of the truth of which they are convinced, then there should be no more fighting.[1]

Mr. Ali must know that Mohammed meant exactly the reverse: Fighting must continue until Islam is the only religion left in the Arabian peninsula. Freedom of religion is one of the victims lying dead in the sand. Like many other Muslim apologists, Ali is little more than a spin doctor following Mohammed with whitewash and brush. He seeks to make even Mohammed's most bigoted statements sound tolerant.

Indeed, Mohammed frequently advocated forced conversion under the guise of what has grown to be Islam's understanding of self-defense.

The twisted logic runs like this: Both the Koran and the hadiths effectively divide all of mankind into two camps. Muslim commentators call them the "House of Islam" and the "House of War."[2] Translation: Anyone who is not a Muslim is assumed to be rejecting Islam. Rejecting Islam equates to *attacking* Islam, Mohammed and even God. Attacking Islam makes one its enemy. Thus war against any non-Muslim under any *feasible* circumstance qualifies as self-defense and is condoned in both the Koran and the hadiths. This explains how Islam, in spite of the Koran's 109 verses written to incite Muslims to commit violence against non-Muslims (see appendix B), can still be called "a religion of peace." It is indeed a religion of peace, but only on the basis of these very vicious terms laid down in the Koran. *That* is the ominous catch.

In other words, Islam's "we fight only in self-defense" claim, even if true in their own minds, actually offers zero assurance to non-Muslims. *Osama bin Laden does indeed have an instructor for his violence, and his name is Mohammed.*

In other passages, Mohammed enjoins war without bothering to mention self-defense as a prerequisite. War to decimate infidel populations by genocide or enslavement is condoned. Turkish Muslims could have quoted the following verse, for example, to justify their mass slaughter of some 1 million Armenian Christians in eastern Turkey in the early 1900s: **"Strike off their heads. Strike off their finger-tips! . . . because they defied God and his Apostle" (Koran 8:12-13)**. Note how this on-paper call to *behead* infidels was accompanied by the very deed against Medinan Jewish men. And did they use physical force to oppose God? No. They just rejected Mohammed's message, as they had every right to do.

Some Muslim translators, M. M. Ali included, try to soften Mohammed's savagery with **"Smite . . . the necks . . . and every finger-tip."** Since the sword was then the primary weapon for smiting, what are we to imagine? Partial decapitation? Fingertips gashed, but still dangling? How reassuring!

Muslim apologists evasively insist that Mohammed's command to perpetrate violence given in 8:12-13 related only to one battle—the Battle of Badr. This presents a problem: This part of the Koran was written *after* the Battle of Badr. How strange that a leader would give his troops instructions as to what to do in a battle *after it had been fought*!

Positing that Mohammed dictated 8:12-13 *prophetically* in anticipation of the Battle of Badr also fails! Kab bin Malik's contemporary testimony, recorded in Sahih al-Bukhari's hadith, entry book 5, volume 59, number 287, repeated in book 5, volume 59, number 702, records that "Allah's Apostle had gone out [with only 300 armed men] to meet [i.e., plunder] the caravans [they were virtually unarmed; hence 300 men would easily be able to overpower and loot them] . . . but Allah caused them (i.e. Muslims) to meet their enemy [a large intervening force from Mecca] *unexpectedly*" (emphasis added).[3]

Kab is making a point: Muslim men who failed to go out to battle with their prophet were normally blamed for their absence. But no one, including Kab himself, was blamed for not being at Badr, because everyone—including the prophet—was taken by surprise! It was supposed to be another easy raid.

M. M. Ali, in his comment number 980, denies that Mohammed intended to raid that unarmed caravan. He let it pass by, Ali would have us believe, and waited several days, preferring to engage the much larger Meccan force. Kab's contemporary testimony exposes Ali's comment as another brushstroke of whitewash.

Mohammed's own words leave no doubt. He was exploiting particulars of the Badr situation to incite Muslims in general to extreme belligerence. And just *what* was Mohammed's justification for urging his followers to behead and maim non-Muslims? **"Because they defied God and his Apostle" (Koran 8:13).**

Actually the Meccans, forewarned of Mohammed's plan, came out merely to protect that unarmed caravan. That of course meant that they **"defied God and his Apostle"**! Radicals like Osama bin Laden know that Mohammed's opponents at Badr are not the only ones who, by Mohammed's definition, are guilty of **"opposing God and his Apostle."**

Rodwell's translation follows with **"*Who so shall* oppose God and his Apostle, God** [i.e., Mohammed] . . . **will punish"** (**Koran 8:13,** emphasis added). Notice that Mohammed generalizes. He gives no assurance that philosophical opposition is to be tolerated and that only *physical* opposition to Islam triggers God's wrath.

This is not self-defense as the civilized world understands it. This is decapitating people because they refuse to believe that God would send a person like Mohammed to represent Him. Again, in 8:40, comes Mohammed's recurring mandate: **"Make war on them** [the infidels] **until idolatry shall cease and God's religion shall reign supreme" (Koran,** see also 2:193 where this verse is repeated word for word**)**. Again, Mohammed extrapolates from the particulars of one literal battle to an equally literal long-term and worldwide one. He gave not the slightest hint that he intended his brutal orders to suggest something analogous to spiritual warfare.

Here is another verse that shows Mohammed eagerly anticipating any number of future battles:

> **Prophet! Rouse the faithful to arms. If there are twenty steadfast men among you they shall vanquish two-hundred; and if there are a hundred, they shall rout a thousand unbelievers. . . . A prophet may not take captives until he has fought and triumphed in the land (Koran 8:65,68).**

Rodwell renders the final phrase of this verse as **"until he has made a great slaughter in the earth" (Koran 8:66,68)**. Another notable verse:

> **Do not befriend [hypocrites] until they have fled their homes in the cause of God (Koran 4:89).**

In other words, "Do not befriend hypocrites until you, fighting in God's cause, have *driven* them from their homes—as Muslims in Medina drove most of the Medinan Jews from their homes." This of course invites a curious question: Why would hypocrites want Muslims to be their friends after Muslims have driven them from their homes? The verse next tells Muslims what to do if any fleeing hypocrites turn around, ostensibly to return to their homes:

Seize them and put them to death wherever you find them (Koran 4:89).

Were nearby neighbors of Muslims immune? Absolutely not!

Believers, make war on the infidels who dwell around you (Koran 9:123).

That was Mohammed's good-neighbor policy toward non-Muslims. Another verse incites:

When you meet the unbelievers in the battlefield strike off their heads and, when you have laid them low, bind your captives firmly (Koran 47:4).

Mohammed is urging his followers to do to unbelievers in general what he did to the Jews in Medina. **"Fighting is obligatory for you, much as you dislike it" (Koran 2:216)** is yet another generalization.

Frequent media reports tell of Muslims forcing non-Muslims to convert to Islam at the muzzle of an AK-47.[4] Muslim apologists are quick to say such reports must be false because Mohammed himself commanded, **"There shall be no compulsion in religion" (Koran 2:257)**. Surely that is a peace verse in the Koran.

Not really. Muslims who quote 2:257 also know that it has been *abrogated* (i.e., annulled, cancelled, replaced) by the very one who initially gave it—the Muslims' God—in at least 109 other verses. Remember, the Muslim doctrine allows God (Mohammed actually) to affirm something positive and then abrogate it with something negative. This is what makes it difficult—impossible really—for us to trust any *good* verse any Muslim apologist ever quotes from the Koran.

Islam allows God to affirm something positive and then abrogate it with something negative.

Indeed, Mohammed permitted no compulsion in his religion—no compulsion, that is, to have to honor his own no-compulsion edict! Note how freely he discards his own insincere assurance of no compulsion in the following quote, which threatens death to idolaters unless they convert:

> **When the sacred months** [the month called Ramadan, year after year] **are over slay the idolaters wherever you find them. Arrest them; besiege them; and lie in ambush everywhere for them. If they repent** ["convert" in Rodwell] **and take to prayer and render the alms levy, allow them to go their way (Koran 9:5).**

Mohammed commanded the forced conversion of idolaters. Did he also command the same for Jews and Christians? One verse seems to indicate that he would never contemplate such a thing. Early in his career as a so-called prophet, Mohammed quotes God as advising him **"If you doubt what We have revealed to you, ask those** [Jews and Christians] **who have read the Scriptures** [the Bible] **before you" (Koran 10:94).**

Initially, Mohammed supposed that Jews and Christians would welcome him as the prophet he claimed to be. When they almost unanimously rejected his claim, he turned in utter rage against those who spurned him. Pretending to quote God verbatim, Mohammed threatened recalcitrant Jews and Christians to convert or else:

> **You to whom the Scriptures were given! Believe in that which We have revealed, confirming your own Scriptures, before We obliterate your faces and turn them backward** [twist your heads around backward]**, or lay Our curse on you (Koran 4:47).**

Only two of seven translators of the Koran felt sheepish enough to try to refine Mohammed's depiction of God as a face eraser and a neck-breaking head twister trying to force Jews and Christians to convert to Islam. In their wording, God threatens to destroy only Jewish and Christian leaders, not the upper extremity of every Jew and Christian's body. What a relief!

Again, in chapter 9, Mohammed raged:

> **Fight against such of those to whom the Scriptures were given [Jews and Christians] as believe [not] in God . . . who do not forbid what God and his Apostle have forbidden** [for example, Mohammed forbade proclaiming the Deity of Jesus as God's Son. See 5:17]**, and do not embrace the true faith until they** [any who survive the war mentioned at the beginning of the verse] **pay tribute out of hand and are utterly subdued (Koran 9:29).**

No compulsion in Mohammed's religion indeed!

The Koran claims that it is God's purpose to **"test the faithful** and annihilate the infidels" (Koran 3:141) and "seek out the enemy relentlessly" (Koran 4:104). The phrase "Fight in the cause of God" (Koran 4:74) recurs again and again almost word for word. All of this is but a sampling of at least 109 verses *advocating religious war* from chapters 2 to 73!

Many other verses in the Koran mention the *plunder* Mohammed and his fellow thieves accumulated with God's total complicity. Here are two:

God promised you rich booty and has given you this with all promptness . . . and God knows of other spoils which you have not yet taken (Koran 48:20-21).

What could be better for a robber gang than to have an omniscient leader? Next:

The spoils belong to God and the Apostle (Koran 8:1).

Forty-one verses later, Islam's God decided that claiming *all* the spoils for himself and Mohammed was greedy, so he had a change of heart: **"Know that one-fifth of our spoils shall belong to God, [and] his Apostle"** (Koran 8:41).

Alas for Mohammed's followers, as the plunder theme keeps recurring in the Koran, the limitation of a 20-percent take for God and Mohammed sometimes gets summarily dropped. For example: **"The spoils taken from the town dwellers and assigned by God to his Apostle shall belong to God, to the Apostle. . . . Whatever the Apostle gives you, accept it. And whatever he forbids you, abstain from it"** (Koran 59:7).

Mohammed commanded, **"As for the man or woman who is guilty of theft, cut off their hands to punish them for their crimes"** (Koran 5:38). His command—which of course he never applied to himself—is still a component of Islam's Sharia law today. Yet Mohammed still authorized his own followers to enter other people's empty homes and perhaps even to steal on the quiet; i.e., apart from raiding: **"There shall be no harm in your entering [unoccupied] houses . . . for the supply of your needs" (Koran 24:29, *Rodwell*).**

Mohammed authorized his followers to enter other people's empty homes and perhaps even to steal on the quiet.

M. Z. Khan's rendering seeks to cover for Mohammed with **"wherein are *your* goods."** Dawood hedges with **"to seek shelter."** M. M. Ali and M. H. Shakir render it ambiguously: **"wherein you have your necessaries."** Arberry is just as vague: **"wherein enjoyment is for you."** Ahmed Ali stands closest to Rodwell with **"where there is some convenience for you."** The more controversial the verse, the more diverse the renderings!

Another issue was how Muslims should treat apostates— those who joined Islam and then reverted back to Judaism, Christianity or idolatry. M. M. Ali writes, "They were named and asked to leave the mosque"—nothing more.[5] But many hadith passages disagree. Sahih al-Bukhari writes that Ali, a contemporary of Mohammed, had Muslims who became atheists "burned alive."[6] Ibn Abbas objected, writing that Mohammed said punishing by fire was reserved for Allah, but even so he "would have killed them according to the statement of Allah's apostle, 'Whoever changed his Islamic religion, then kill him.'"[7] Yet Mohammed, referring to people who **"renounced Islam after** embracing it" **(Koran 9:74)** has God urging him to **"make war"** **(Koran 9:73)** on them.

In Bukhari book 9, volume 84, number 58, read about a Muslim named Muadh who slew a Jew who reverted from Islam. In Bukhari book 9, volume 84, number 64, rewards are promised to any who slay apostates.

Mohammed even had Muslims who confessed hidden sin stoned to death. In Bukhari book 8, volume 82, read numbers 805, 806, 809, 813, 814, 815, 821 and 842 and shudder!

Notes

1. Maulana Muhammad Ali, *Quran* (Columbus, OH: Lahore, Inc., USA, 1998), comment 244.
2. Ibn Warraq, *Why I Am Not a Muslim* (Amherst, NY: Prometheus Books, 1995), p. 218.
3. Sahih al-Bukhari, *Translation of Sahih Bukhari* (*The Book of Knowledge*), trans. Mohammed Muhsin Khan, book 5, vol. 59, no. 287 and book 5, vol. 59, no. 702, *University of Southern California*, http://www.usc.edu/dept/MSA/fundamentals/hadithsunnah/bukhari/059.sbt.html (accessed October 25, 2002).
4. "Forced Conversions to Islam Continue in Indonesia," *Worthy News*, http://www.worthynews.com/news-features/indonesia-ethnic-cleansing-8.html (accessed January 13, 2001).
5. Ali, *Quran*, comments 1067 and 1080.
6. al-Bukhari, *Sahih Bukhari*, book 9, vol. 84, no. 57.
7. Ibid.

CRITIQUING THE KORAN

Some readers will protest that a book revered as sacred by more than 1 billion people should *not be critiqued*—unless the conclusions drawn are entirely positive. It is the old "if you can't say something *nice*, don't say anything" bromide. That may be good counsel for social *tête-à-tête*. It is bad advice when dealing with a book that is—in the hands of hundreds of millions of Muslims who honor it today—potentially a threat to world peace.

Alas, with the attacks of September 11, 2001, and a thousand related events across the world, the literary gloves must come off. The Koran has received much criticism over the centuries, but there have been few scholarly reviews.

EYE-OPENING EXAMINATIONS

One of the first to examine the Koran in depth was Sir William Muir's *Muhammad*, last republished in 1923. There was also Maxime Rodinson's *Muhammad* in 1961. Then came a number of liberal-minded authors—W. Montgomery Watt and Karen Armstrong among them—who listened much too naively to newly emerging Muslim apologists. Persuaded that Mohammed had been unjustly demonized, they set forth to correct the perceived injustice. Alas, in their pursuit they are unable to refute the record of historical perfidy from Islam's own sources. Several set out by professing a desire to refute an unfair demonization of Mohammed, but only ended up confirming that no one needed to demonize him—he was quite skilled at demonizing himself.

Now, when objective reviews of the Koran are so needed, Muir and Rodinson are long out of print and largely forgotten.

Mohammed According to the Historians

A few briefer critiques from the past mention Mohammed's murderous deeds only in passing, choosing to focus mainly on the relatively unimportant matter of his notably uncommendable literary style. For example, Edward Gibbon, in his *Decline and Fall of the Roman Empire*, wrote:

> [The Koran is an] incoherent rhapsody of fable and precept and declamation which seldom excites a sentiment or an idea, which sometimes crawls in the dust and is sometimes lost in the clouds. . . . The use of fraud and perfidy, of cruelty and injustice, were often subservient to the propagation of the faith, . . . Mohammed commanded or approved the assassination of Jews and idolaters, . . . Mohammed indulged the appetites of a man and abused the claims of a prophet. A special

revelation dispensed him from the laws which he had imposed upon his nation. The female sex, without reserve, was abandoned to his desires.[1]

A later chapter will detail what Gibbon was describing in his last sentence.

Thomas Carlyle, in *Sartor Resartus: On Heroes and Hero Worship*, described the Koran as:

A wearisome jumble, crude, incondite [with] endless iterations [and] longwindedness. . . . Nothing but a sense of duty could carry any European through the Koran.[2]

Philosopher David Hume, in his *An Enquiry Concerning Human Understanding*, commented:

[Mohammed] bestows praise upon such instances of treachery, inhumanity, cruelty, revenge and bigotry as are utterly incompatible with civilized society. No steady rule of right seems there to be attended to, and every action is blamed or praised so far only as it is beneficial or hurtful to the true believers.[3]

Recent Reviewers

In recent years a few free-thinking *Muslim* intellectuals have openly criticized the Koran. Salman Rushdie's *The Satanic Verses* does not stand alone, although such commentary has been quite hard to find throughout Muslim history. Iranian Ali Dashti reviewed the 23 years of Mohammed's so-called prophetic career in a book titled *Twenty-Three Years: A Study of the Prophetic Career of Mohammad*. Dashti found not only the content but even the literary style of Mohammed's original Arabic to be seriously defective. Dashti complained:

The Koran contains sentences [in the Arabic original] which are incomplete and unintelligible without . . . commentaries. Foreign words . . . and words used with other than the normal meaning, [words] inflected without the concord of gender and number, illogically and ungrammatically applied pronouns which sometimes have no referent, and predicates which in rhymed passages are often remote from their subjects . . . more than 100 Koranic aberrations from [Arabic's] normal rules have been noted.[4]

Toby Lester, reviewing critical scholarship on the Koran for the *Atlantic Monthly*, quotes the opinion of a German scholar who is so skilled in Arabic that Yemen entrusted to him the analysis of extremely old copies of the Koran found in a Yemeni mosque. His name is Gerd R. Puin. He comments:

The Koran claims for itself that it is *"mubeen"* or "clear." But if you look at it [in the original Arabic, as Puin does], you will notice that every fifth sentence or so simply doesn't make sense. Many Muslims—and Orientalists—will tell you otherwise, of course, but the fact is that a fifth of the Koranic text is *just incomprehensible*. This is what had caused the traditional anxiety regarding translation. If the Koran is not comprehensible—if it can't even be understood in Arabic—then it's not translatable. People fear that [fact]. And since the Koran claims repeatedly to be clear but obviously is not—as even speakers of Arabic will tell you—there is a contradiction. Something else is going on.[5]

Another book-length scathing critique, *Why I Am Not a Muslim,* authored by a former Muslim, Ibn Warraq, appeared in

1995. As a $30 hardcover, it has not reached a wide audience. It also has a major flaw. Warraq, obviously unsettled by the religion he knows best—Islam—overextends, asserting that "all religions are sick men's dream."[6]

Just off the press in 2002—the English translation of British-Egyptian author Bat Ye'or's *Islam and Dhimmitude: Where Civilizations Collide* (see bibliography). Her 500-plus pages masterfully dismantle several centuries of effort by Muslims to dignify Islam's 1,400 years of abuse of Jews, Christians and Zoroastrians in the Middle East. Ye'or finds the roots of that extremely intense and protracted abuse embedded in the Koran itself. Mohammed cannot plead innocence due to misinterpretation by his followers.

REASONS FOR THIS BOOK

In this book, I attempt to condense as succinctly as possible major insights from Muir, Rodinson, Warraq and Ye'or. I also add other truths regarding the Koran that even *they* missed. September 11, 2001, raised mankind's need for an objective yet concise critique of the Koran to the highest level of priority.

Every quote I use from the Koran has been compared in eight versions.

It has taken strong conviction to draw me to this research. I have friends who are Muslims. That they and others may know that I write with care, I have seven different translations of the Koran on my desk and an eighth on my computer screen. Six are the work of Muslim scholars. As I noted in the preface, every quote I use from the Koran has been compared in all eight versions, lest one translator's error would cause me to misread Mohammed's intent.

DANGER IN THE MADRASAS

The world needs to be warned. At least 40 million Muslim youth in the Muslim world's religious schools, called madrasas, are avidly memorizing the entire Koran plus a generally extremist body of related traditions—the hadiths. In the hands of extremists—whether run by Saudi Wahabbists, Osama bin Laden's followers or Indonesian mullahs—these schools become breeding grounds for potential terrorists. Early in the

> **Uncounted throngs of madrasa students are wearing Osama bin Laden T-shirts. Radical clerics have made him their hero.**

training, Muslim teachers especially focus pliable young minds on dozens of the Koran's extremely militant *war verses,* plus other texts that assure paradise for Muslim *martyrs.* Hatred for Jews and Christians (largely synonymous with Israel and America) and general disdain for *all* non-Muslims (defined by Muslim instructors as the House of War) are deeply instilled.[7] The Bible is described as corrupted. Separation of Islam from political control is despised.

When male students, isolated from family and friends in *madrasas,* reach puberty and their hormones are active, there are no girls to date. Instead, Muslim clerics easily shift to focusing the male students' attention on Koranic verses that promise sex in heaven with dark-eyed houris (see chapter 3). Students can only fantasize about martyrdom followed by the sexual release Mohammed promised. This is an unspeakably cruel brainwashing technique, and the Koran is its perfect guidebook. Uncounted throngs of madrasa students are wearing Osama bin Laden T-shirts. Radical clerics have made him their hero.

Simply put, 40 million trainees in Muslim madrasas are a societal nuclear bomb, and the Koran's war and sex verses are the U-235 inside. Consider the following warning by Jeffrey Goldberg in *Reader's Digest*:

> East of the Kyber Pass, in the North-West frontier province of Pakistan, sits a school called the Haqqania madrassa. . . . The school enrolls more than 2800 male students, drawn mostly from the dire poor. Tuition, room and board are free . . . funded by wealthy Pakistanis and devout, politically minded Muslims in Persian Gulf countries. The students range in age from 8 to 35. The youngest boys spend 4 to 8 hours a day . . . memorizing the Koran in the original Arabic. [Older students] are enrolled in an 8-year course . . . focusing on the interpretation of the Koran and the Hadith (a narration of the life and sayings of the Prophet Muhammed), Islamic jurisprudence and Islamic history. There are no courses here in world history, English, math, computers or science. . . . The Haqqania madrassa is, in fact, a jihad factory. . . . [In one class] I asked, "Who wants to see bin Laden armed with nuclear weapons?" Every hand in the room shot up. . . . "What would you do if . . . the CIA . . . captured bin Laden and was taking him to America?" A student named Muhammed stood up: "We would sacrifice our lives for Osama. We would kill Americans."[8]

Goldberg writes that 1 million Muslim students fill 10,000 madrasas in Pakistan alone. He concludes: "These are poor and impressionable boys kept entirely ignorant of the world and, for that matter, largely ignorant of all but one interpretation of Islam. They are perfect jihad machines."[9] Myriad other madrasas that use the Koran as a textbook are found from Senegal to the southern Philippines. Some are now opening in America and other Western nations.

Professor Mochtar Buchori, a member of the Indonesian Parliament, reported on July 1, 2002, via Indonesia's Laksamana.net, on the madrasa situation in Indonesia, a nation of more than 200 million Muslims.[10]

To grasp Buchori's figures, consider this: If we add all the universities, colleges, high schools, junior high schools and elementary schools in the United States, we find the total is about 24,000 institutions. Yet Buchori counts *37,362 Muslim madrasas in Indonesia alone!* Of these only 8 percent have any input from Indonesia's government. In 92 percent, the teaching agenda is controlled by Muslim clerics. Buchori warns that 4.6 million Indonesian students are enrolled in the privately run madrasas. He further cautions that government offers to provide courses teaching math, English and science are strongly rejected by most private madrasas. He concludes that the potential for a majority of such schools to train terrorists is high.

A Clear Signal

A world crisis is brewing. A spotlight must be turned on. This critique is surely only part of a massive *deeper* investigation of the Koran that recent events require. The Koran is not someone's private mail. It is a published book offered to the world as inspired by God. The world has a right to examine it square on. Let us do exactly that.

Mohammed himself declared, **"Who is more wicked than the man who . . . says, 'This was revealed to me,' when nothing was revealed to him?" (Koran 6:93).** It is time for the world to know who Mohammed was best describing.

Notes

1. Edward Gibbon, *The Decline and Fall of the Roman Empire*, vol. 5 (New York: Random House, 1994), n.p.
2. Thomas Carlyle, *Sartor Resartus: On Heroes and Hero Worship* (London: J. M. Dent and Sons, Ltd., 1967), n.p.
3. David Hume, *An Enquiry Concerning Human Understanding*, ed. Tom L. Beauchamp (Oxford, England: Oxford University Press, 1999), n.p.
4. Ali Dashti, *Twenty-Three Years: A Study of the Prophetic Career of Mohammad*, trans. F. R. C. Bagley (Costa Mesa, CA: Mazda Publishers, 1994), n.p.
5. Toby Lester, "What Is the Koran?: For People Who Understand," January 1999, *The Atlantic Monthly*, http://www/theatlantic.com/issues/99jan/koran3.thm (accessed September 29, 2002). Used by permission.
6. Ibn Warraq, *Why I Am Not a Muslim* (Amherst, NY: Prometheus Books, 1995), p. xiii.
7. Ibid., p. 218.
8. Jeffrey Goldberg, "The Making of a Terrorist," *Reader's Digest*, January 2002, pp. 70-75, condensed from *New York Times Magazine*.
9. Ibid.
10. Mochtar Buchori, Laksamana.net (accessed August 24, 2002).

CHAPTER FIVE

POLYGAMY AND ISLAM'S PROPHET

Along with the plunder and ransom money Mohammed and his followers amassed were captive *women*. What rules did he give to govern the behavior of male captors with their female captives?

Mohammed knew that men who are responsible for female orphans, let alone feminine slaves, might be tempted to violate them sexually. He advised men thus tempted to marry **"other women . . . two, three or four of them" (Koran 4:3)** to help them keep their thoughts distracted from comely young adoptees. Note that *two* is the minimum number Mohammed suggested. Monogamy, apparently, was not even to be considered. And because Mohammed mentioned four, everywhere in the world that Islam's Sharia law supercedes other laws, Muslim men are permitted four wives.

M. M. Ali, eager to excuse Mohammed's failure to urge self-control or monogamy instead of polygamy as a solution for male temptation, assures monogamous Western readers: "This passage permits polygamy under certain circumstances; it does not enjoin it."[1] If that is true, why couldn't at least one wife be listed in 4:3 as one of the options? Still, in spite of Mohammed's failure even to mention monogamy in 4:3 as acceptable, Ali wants us to believe that the Koran favors calling human societies away from polygamy toward monogamy. Does it?

Polygamy for the strong, monogamy for the weak is clearly Mohammed's policy!

Again Mohammed, claiming to speak as God's voice, side-steps his defender's effort to improve his image, instructing: **"But if you fear you cannot treat so many with equity, marry only one, or a maid or captive" (Koran 4:3, *Ahmed Ali*)**. So, finally—but only as an afterthought—Mohammed *does* recommend monogamy, but only if a particular Muslim male has some sort of personality problem that prevents him from treating more than one wife "with equity." Polygamy for the strong, monogamy for the weak is clearly Mohammed's policy!

Dawood renders the concluding phrase in the above quote: **"Or any slave girls** [again note the persistent plural] **you may own."** M. M. Ali, Shakir and Arberry translate: **"Or that which**

your right hands possess." The latter all knew that many Western readers would not recognize that phrase as an Arab euphemism for "slave girls."

What kind of disincentive for polygamy is that? What kind of disincentive is that for slavery!

MOHAMMED, MARRIAGE AND SLAVES

Mohammed appears to have lived a morally circumspect life as a youth. At 25 he married a woman 15 years his senior and remained monogamously married to her for 25 years. She died three years before his flight from Mecca to Medina. In the eyes of his followers, Mohammed was living evidence that male self-control can coexist with monogamy. Why did he not make his own initial monogamous self-control an example for his followers?

Something within Mohammed must have snapped.

In Mecca, Mohammed was not violent, nor was he a robber or polygamist. In Medina, by his own choice, he became all three and more. A man known for self-control is even more contemptible if he abandons self-control than a man who lived as a rake and a scoundrel from his youth.

What were Mohammed's reasons for changing? Every indicator following Mohammed's arrival in Medina points to his decision to build up a fighting force that would not only plunder Mecca's caravans and expel or kill Medina's Jews, but also eventually be large enough to defeat the hostile Arabs who expelled him from his hometown, Mecca. Prescribing his original monogamy as a standard for pagan men would, of course, have turned away many a pagan man Mohammed coveted for a rapid buildup of his fighting force. Or did he feel that 25 years of monogamy in Mecca earned him the right just to live it up in Medina?

How did Mohammed's transition from monogamy to polygamy occur?

Not long before Mohammed was expelled from Mecca, an admirer brought his six-year-old daughter, Aisha, and offered to marry her to Mohammed. Mohammed accepted. One wonders first of all what strange logic—or lack of the same—would motivate a father to truncate his little girl's childhood so drastically. Just as critical is a second question: How could a man claiming to be a prophet of God fail to show sane restraint by accepting such an off-the-wall offer from an obviously confused, misled or delinquent parent? It does not excuse Mohammed to say "that sort of thing was Arab custom." Surely God sends his prophets not to conform to human folly but to replace folly with wisdom.

Mohammed kept adding wife after wife to his harem—all with Allah's full consent.

Muslim tradition claims that Mohammed, for an obvious reason, did not consummate this, his second marriage, until Aisha was nine years of age. The question remains: How many times did he try to consummate his marriage to a mere child during the first three years? Mohammed left himself open to suspicion of pedophilia.

A Change of Heart
Perhaps it was that three years of inability to have sex with little Aisha that drove Mohammed to add another wife to her, at which point he became a polygamist and there was no turning back. He kept adding wife after wife to his harem—all with

Allah's full consent. Mohammed's God was fully compliant. Whatever the new nonmonogamous Mohammed wanted, his God was eager to grant. Note the following *carte blanche* divine endorsement that Mohammed's Koran gives to Mohammed:

> **Prophet! We** ["we" means "God"] **have made lawful for you the wives to whom you have granted dowries and the slave girls whom God has given you as booty; the daughters of your paternal and maternal uncles and of your paternal and maternal aunts . . . and any believing woman who gives herself to the Prophet and whom the Prophet wishes to take in marriage. This privilege is yours alone, being granted to no other believer. . . . [We grant you this privilege] so that none may blame you. . . . You may . . . take to your bed any of them you please"** (Koran 33:50-51).

Then, as if feeling sheepish after such an impulsive outburst of doting indulgence, the Muslim God cautioned:

> **[After this] it shall be unlawful for you to take more wives or to change your present wives for other women, though their beauty please you (Koran 33:52).**

Why does a holy prophet need to be publicly warned to avoid wife-trading? But wait—there is more! Lest Mohammed feel miffed to have to endure even the above-mentioned minimal limitation, his God is suddenly indulgent again, adding an oh-so-generous *unless* **"they are slave girls whom you own" (Koran 33:52).**

Any time Mohammed wanted to add spice to his sex life, all he had to do was raid another town or caravan for female slaves, or buy some, and his God would approve. So, in fact, for him there really was no limit.

Verse 33:50, interestingly, admits a need to shield Mohammed from *blame* for having sex with so many women. Obviously *someone* sensed that common conscience, unless somehow anesthetized, *would* indeed condemn his excess as wrong, even among his own followers. Therefore, if moral standards must be lowered to make a leader's abnormality appear right, who better than God, inventor of morality, to lower the standard?

Concerning "God" and Mohammed, one wonders which was the servant and which was the master? Mohammed reduced his God virtually to the level of a procurer, a mere auxiliary to himself.

Rules for Making a Female Slave an "Honest Woman"

Occasionally a Muslim man would decide that a captive woman whom Mohammed had given him to use as a sex slave should be his wife instead. Chapter 4 in Mohammed's Koran lays down three conditions that had to be fulfilled before a mere slave could be the wife of a Muslim man. M. M. Ali lists them:

1. The slave must be a believer (see Koran 4:25).
2. A man must persuade the community that he cannot afford the bride price for a free woman (see Koran 4:25).
3. The man is afraid he will fall into sin if he does not marry that pretty slave.[2]

All a male Muslim need do is admit a little weakness. Could this be the reason their God had to cater so obeisantly to Mohammed's desire for sex?

In Chapter 70 of the Koran, Mohammed invited male Muslims to descend to the same lower marital standard his God had already authorized for *him*. First, though, posing as a guard for morality, Mohammed commended male Muslims who **"control their desires" (Koran 70:29, *Rodwell*)**. Then he added indulgently, **"Save with their wives and slave girls; for these are lawful for them" (Koran 70:30;** see also 23:5). The slaves mentioned in these two verses are not included in the category of wives.

M. M. Ali writes, "I do not find any verse [in the Koran] sanctioning what is called *concubinage*."[3] Yet I have just listed two.

What is Mohammed really saying? *Control* your sexual desires because God is granting you greater opportunity to *indulge* them? Again, this absolution from "blame" (see Koran 33:52) reveals Mohammed's awareness of a higher moral standard and his deliberate intent to lower it.

Of course, a majority of Muslims do not want to harm non-Muslims.

Of course, a majority of Muslims do not want to harm non-Muslims. Unlike their so-called prophet, *they* do not plunder other people's homes nor do they exploit female captives as sex slaves. God forbid that any reader of this critique of the Koran should think that Muslims must be punished for being misled by a bad prophet and his bad book. May God defend people in every nation from vigilante justice—including Muslims in Western nations and Christians and other minorities in Muslim nations!

In fact, moderate Muslims can be commended for living on a much higher ethical plane than the so-called prophet they have been taught to honor. But why should anyone be taught in the first place to honor as a prophet a man whom any discerning person would utterly disdain if unlucky enough actually to meet him?

Polygamy in the Bible?

Several Old Testament notables—David and Solomon, for example—were polygamists. God, except in 2 Samuel 12:8, where He tells David through the prophet Nathan that He gave David his wives, was silent, perhaps letting Old Testament polygamists exercise, in their age of relative societal immaturity, what Jesus, referring to divorce, would later call *hardness of heart* (see Mark 10:5). Jesus, on the other hand, had much to say. In Matthew 19:4-9, He said, "*the* two *will become one flesh*" (emphasis added), not the three, four or five, affirming that one man should have only one wife. The Judeo-Christian God took *one* rib from Adam's side. The God of Islam—the God who is eager to smother every faithful Muslim man with dozens of houris in paradise—would have taken three or four (or perhaps even left poor Adam *ribless*).

Surely there is no affirmation of the equality of male and female that is more convincing than monogamy! The apostle Paul profoundly reinforces the primacy of monogamy in 1 Corinthians 7 and 1 Timothy 3:2. Why would Mohammed's God—touted by Mohammed as *confirming* the New Testament—so effusively authorize polygamy, overriding both Jesus and Paul?

Ruth 3:12 reveals that even the kinsman-redeemer law from Deuteronomy 25:5 did not require an already-married man to wed a deceased brother's childless widow. Boaz, though second in line, married Ruth, his brother's childless widow, because if she had married the man who was first in line, the marriage would have "endangered the estate" for his own children. Since there is no mention of Boaz already having a wife, we surmise that he was either a bachelor or a widower.

How Muslims Justify Mohammed's Polygamy

How do Muslim apologists defend Mohammed's polygamy? The previous quotes show that for Mohammed himself, "God let me do it" was defense enough. M. M. Ali, ever ready to strengthen what Mohammed left weak, adds a reason Mohammed and his God both forgot to give 1,400 years earlier in the Koran. Ali claims that Muslim male casualties in battle left many women widowed. Mohammed prescribed polygamy, Ali suggests, because so many widows needed care and there were no single men to wed them. Yet Mohammed forbade anyone to wed any of the numerous widows that he would leave when *he* died (see Koran 33:53b). And what about the slave girls with whom Mohammed had sex? They were not widows. What kind of special care did they need, prompting Mohammed to have sex with them? In Koran 4:3 it is caution or the lack of self-control, not an excess of widows, that prompted the authorization of polygamy.

In discussions about polygamy in Islam, occasionally someone jibes: "Men like it; women hate it." But polygamy, realistically appraised, is a curse for both sexes. Here is why: In polygamous cultures, married men with daughters yield to the temptation to form *de facto* daughter-trading clubs. One says to a fellow polygamist: "I will give you my daughter to be your third wife, but only if you give me your daughter as my fourth wife." Where does that leave single men? Vehemently resenting the greed, the avarice of already-married males. Single men have little option but to entice or steal a bride and elope—a cause of endless rancor, feuding and bloodshed. Relativist sophisms fail. *Polygamy is a curse for men and women both!*

Ever so many cultures throughout history have had an excess of widows following wars, but have not found it advisable to resort to polygamy for their care.

HOW MOHAMMED TOOK STILL ANOTHER WIFE

Jesus raised the dead; Mohammed killed the living. Jesus healed the sick; Mohammed harmed the healthy. Jesus released the oppressed; Mohammed enslaved the free. Jesus sanctified Earth with that which is heavenly; Mohammed sullied mankind's under-standing of heaven with the earthly.

In fact, Mohammed could not even reach up to touch the underside of the moral standards of an average rogue.

Mohammed and His Daughter-In-Law

Consider this story I have paraphrased from several sources: When Mohammed already possessed several wives and who knows how many slave girls, his own adopted son and favorite right-hand man, Zaid ibn Haritha, married lovely Zaynab. Zaynab was Zaid's only bride. She was in her mid-30s, a few years older than Zaid.

One day the so-called messenger of Allah came to pay a visit. Zaid was not at home. Zaynab came to the door in a state of rel-ative undress. Modestly stepping behind a curtain to clothe her-self more appropriately, Zaynab asked Mohammed in. Muslim sources in the hadiths almost delight in describing how the wind lifted the curtain a little, and Mohammed was smitten—if he wasn't already—by Zaynab's beauty. Zaynab heard Mohammed exclaim, "Praise be to Allah, the Most High! Praise be to Allah who changes men's hearts!"

Whose heart did Mohammed seem to *know* was already changed? Had Zaid wearied of Zaynab or otherwise struck some strange deal with his foster father? Was Mohammed there to appraise his end of a bargain?

Mohammed left excitedly. When Zaid learned of his foster father's emotional reaction during the momentary encounter, he seemed to know exactly what he had to do. Or was it all planned? Did he know he would be well reimbursed in plunder or in other women?

A Tempting Offer and a Rebuke

Zaid went directly to Mohammed and offered to divorce Zaynab so she could be added to Mohammed's already well-stocked harem.

Of course, the offer had to be initiated by Zaid. Mohammed must not appear to be actually *stealing* his adopted son's only wife. The great Mohammed could never be seen as immoral.

Mohammed of course protested that Zaid must keep his wife for himself. By then the entire Muslim community was watching. It must have seemed to everyone that the matter was resolved. Mohammed had given Zaid an order. Zaid must keep his wife. No one could overrule a prophet's command.[4]

But wait! Yes, of course, there *was* someone who *could* overrule a prophet's command: *God!*

The Intervention of God

Right on cue, the God of Islam, reduced again to abetting perfidy, sternly reprimanded Mohammed for resisting God's will: **"When you told the man . . . 'Keep your wife,' . . . you were concealing within yourself what Allah was to reveal. You feared men** [public opinion]. **. . . Let Allah's will be done" (Koran 33:37).**[5]

A chastened Mohammed hastily married Zaynab. Rodinson further criticizes Muslim authors and another Western sophist named Montgomery Watt (Karen Armstrong's predecessor, in my view) for trying to argue that Mohammed had no sexual interest in Zaynab. It was, Watt and those like him insisted, only a marriage for political purposes.

Not surprisingly, the remainder of chapter 33 in the Koran musters seven warnings against blame, insolence, speaking ill and scandal-mongering being levied against the Muslim prophet.

Little wonder! In this environment, was there anyone who dared speak freely?

The Words of a Jealous Wife

There was, however, one spectator at this sorry affair who let it be known publicly that she could easily see through Mohammed's charade. That brave person was his understandably

jealous second wife, Aisha. A hadith credits her with enough bold-
ness to be heard saying, in effect: "If any part of that 'revelation'
should have been concealed, it was the part [God] divulged."[6]

Everyone could see plainly that Mohammed's God was ready
to command whatever Mohammed wanted. Evil choices needed
divine cover for propriety's sake.

WOMEN AS SEX OBJECTS?

Finally, in a quote shocking to even a fanatic endorser of the
Koran as "holy," Mohammed commanded:

> **Do not force your slave girls into prostitution in order
> that you may enrich yourselves . . . (Koran 24:33)**

M. M. Ali avers: "Prostitution . . . is condemned here."[7] Mr. Ali,
how wrong you are. As other seemingly moralistic commands of
Mohammed come with an "unless" clause or an "except" clause (exposing them as pseudomoralistic), so this one is followed by an
"if" clause with the same effect. Mohammed added:

> . . . *if* **they** [the slave girls] **wish to preserve their chasti-
> ty (Koran 24:33,** emphasis added**).**

What did Mohammed mean? *If* a slave girl is unconcerned
about chastity, her owner *may* profit by prostituting her! Imagine
how easily a lecherous owner might pressure a slave girl to *say* she
was unconcerned, when in fact she loathed what her owner was
forcing her to do. Hold on. There is more. Mohammed continues
the verse:

> **If anyone** [i.e., any slave owner] **compels them** [forces
> chastity-choosing slave girls to be prostitutes], **God will be
> forgiving and merciful to them (Koran 24:33).**

Slave girls thus compelled had no choice, so they cannot be the "them" needing forgiveness. Mohammed was blatantly committing his God to absolve Muslims who force slave girls into prostitution.

Yet M. M. Ali calls Mohammed "the greatest source of righteousness the world has ever witnessed."[8]

An even more vulgar example of Mohammed's view of captive women as sex objects is found in the hadiths. Bukhari, regarded as a reliable collector of hadiths, quotes an early Muslim, Abu Said al-Khudri, who described what happened when some of Mohammed's male followers came to him with what at first glance resembles a confession, but was actually just a question. The men said:

> We took some women captive and in coition practiced *coitus interruptus*, so as not to have offspring from them. Did we offend Allah?[9]

Most people, of course, would expect Mohammed to rebuke his acolytes, saying something like this: "The issue is not whether *coitus interruptus* offends Allah. What offends Allah is kidnapping and rape!" Alas, Mohammed blithely assures his proteges that *coitus interruptus* is not a problem because anyone Allah intends should exist will exist no matter what. The idea that kidnapping and rape are criminal acts is nowhere in sight! Evidently such crimes were so common under Mohammed's influence that definitions of public morality had been altered to excuse them.

After all this chapter and earlier chapters reveal of extremely objectionable content in the Koran, are there no good verses in it? Indeed, several passages describe nature beautifully. Good advice pops up here and there, such as: **"Be neither miserly nor prodigal, for then you should either earn reproach or be reduced to penury" (Koran 17:29)**. One hundred seventeen verses warn against idolatry, if one is tempted. But the Koran's good verses are like the food an assassin adds to poison to disguise a deadly taste. Better to find the same food, sans poison, in the Bible or even in proverbs, like "Waste not, want not" or "A penny saved is a penny earned."

Islam insists that Muslims accept the Koran in its entirety, so accepting its good verses leads one inexorably to accept also its evil verses—the ones that advocate violence, slavery, sex with slaves and even prostitution.

Notes

1. Maulana Muhammad Ali, *Quran* (Columbus, OH: Lahore, Inc., USA, 1998), comment 535.
2. Ibid., comment 561.
3. Ibid.
4. Maxime Rodinson, *Muhammad* (New York: Pantheon Books, 1971), pp. 204-208.
5. Sahih al-Bukhari, *Translation of Sahih Bukhari* (*The Book of Knowledge*), trans. Mohammed Muhsin Khan, book 93, vol. 9, no. 516, *University of Southern California*, http://www.usc.edu/dept/MSA/fundamentals/hadithsunnah/bukhari/059.sbt.html (accessed October 25, 2002).
6. Rodinson, *Muhammad*, p. 206.
7. Ali, *Quran*, comment 1,756.
8. Ibid., comment 1,998.
9. Sahih al-Bukhari, *Translation of Sahih Bukhari* (*The Book of Knowledge*), trans. Mohammed Muhsin Khan, "Kitab al Jami' al Sahih," *University of Southern California*, http://www.usc.edu/dept/MSA/fundamentals/hadithsunnah/bukhari/059.sbt.html (accessed October 25, 2002).

CHAPTER SIX

HOW MUSLIMS TRY TO DEFEND THE KORAN

In previous chapters I responded to some of Muslim apologist M. M. Ali's attempts to defend various Koranic verses that tend to create difficulties for Islam. Rebutting dozens of his other defenses could easily fill a separate volume. Instead, I now turn to more general arguments that Muslim apologists tend to use to try to justify Islam's vastly overstated claims for the Koran.

Defense 1: The Koran Confirms Itself As Inspired by God to Those Who Approach It with Reverence

Muslims urge everyone who decides to investigate the Koran to feel reverential awe for the book, even before reading it. M. Z. Khan, in a 52-page introduction to his translation of the Koran, warns:

> A student of the Koran must bring certain qualities to his study. . . . The two most important are reverence and humility. The Koran claims to be the Word of God. A non-Muslim reader may not accept this, but he must keep it in mind and must respect it. . . . The Koran reacts towards one who studies it according to his own attitude toward the Koran. If he starts with the assumption that it is a fabrication, his study . . . will confirm his preconceived bias. A student must free his mind from all prejudice. . . . The Koran expects an open mind.[1]

History is filled with books noted for convincing the unconvinced of perspectives previously doubted. Would not a book authored by God rank high in this category? But no, if the Koran does not impress us—even if we find logical flaws and moral indiscretions in it—it is not the Koran's fault, claims Khan. We are to blame.

I think not. A book that claims to be God's Word—among all books—is even *more* to be read with honest doubt. Khan leaves no room for this. Whatever is not reverence he labels as "irreverence," "pride," "preconceived bias" or "prejudice."[2] This is a cultic ploy to try to disarm, confuse and finally *subvert* a potential convert's intellect. Khan's idea of an open mind is actually an empty mind. It is a mind *so open* logic has fallen out.

Defense 2: The Way the Koran Resonates So Beautifully in Arabic Evidences Divine Inspiration

Linked with the weak "begin with reverence" plea is the equally flawed "it [the Koran] sounds so beautiful in Arabic" defense. Muslim apologists rhapsodize, even symphonate, about how poetic, how stirring, the mere sound of the Koran's Arabic is to the ear. Should we take that—even if it were true—as evidence for the Koran's claim to divine inspiration? All such rhetoric has one goal: to distract thoughtful readers from the reality of the Koran's violence, repetitiveness and pseudomoralizing.

No matter how liltingly *Alice in Wonderland* is read, it is still fiction. Likewise, no matter how grandiloquently the Koran is intoned in Arabic, when the meaning is known, it is still a tedious manifesto attempting to justify crimes against humanity.

Defense 3: Seeming Foibles in the Koran Are due to the Inability of Other Languages to Convey What the Koran Expresses in Arabic

Many Muslim apologists often fall back to a third-string defense: "Other languages," they plead, "cannot properly express what the Koran says in Arabic." If only we Westerners could read the Arabic, presumably the repetitions would not be repetitive, the lack of nouns (see defense 4 below) would not confuse and Mohammed's moral lapses and violence would not look objectionable.

They have to say "cannot express," rather than "does not express," because too many English translations of the Koran render the numerous objectionable passages the same or nearly the same way, which is no doubt embarrassing. How could that many translators simply be wrong?

Of course, one must first select a sample problematic verse and then ask a Muslim apologist, "If no translation truly conveys the meaning of the Koran's Arabic, tell us what must be added to make this sample verse nonproblematic?" The apologist then offers in plain English what he claims is missing from the translation, unwittingly refuting his own argument. It leaves him mumbling when we ask, "Why couldn't any of these many translators put it the way you did just now, if the Arabic says what you claim?"

As one who speaks three languages, I attest that—apart from a few subtle idioms or plays on words—there is virtually *nothing* that cannot be translated from any language to any other language! Muslim claims that a wealth of Arabic meaning is sieved out by translation are nonsense (see quotes from Puin and Dashti in chapter 2).

If the Koran makes full sense only in Arabic, it is not a revelation for all mankind.

If the Koran makes full sense only in Arabic, it is not a revelation for all mankind—unless *Allah* (Arabic for "God") requires all mankind to learn Arabic. In fact, teachers in thousands of Muslim madrasas require millions of non-Arab students to memorize the entire Koran *in Arabic*—a language they do not know or understand! Could this be a cover-up? Keen minds that would be bored or appalled by a pseudorevelation *if they could understand it* are left in the dark, knowing only what a mullah—the equivalent of a pastor in Islam—chooses to explain in the local language.

Defense 4: Sans Divine Inspiration, Such a Literary Masterpiece Could Not Come from an Illiterate Man

Millions of people who never open a Koran hear from Muslims that it is a marvelous book. Even some secular scholars extol it.

Grill them, though, and most admit to *browsing* a few pages. Some professors are reticent to say anything that would cause Muslim college students to boycott their classes.

With so much hype praising the Koran, a novice expects to feel inspired as he begins reading. Boredom quickly chills expectation. Mohammed, the illiterate Arabian religious leader who dictated the Koran to various scribes in the early 600s, acknowledged himself as **"unlettered" (Koran 7:157)**. In 7:183 he described his role as **"that of a plain warner" (Koran)**.

An illiterate with limited intellectual horizons—to fill hundreds of bits of parchment with teaching—does indeed need help from a mind better informed than his own. Or, he must rely heavily on repetition just to fill space. Then he has a problem. How can he repeat, repeat, repeat without boring his readers?

That was precisely Mohammed's quandary.

Chapter 1 in the Koran is only eight verses long, hence the main text begins with chapter 2's 286 verses. Readers encounter banal repetition immediately. In verse 7, Mohammed warns non-Muslims about a **"great punishment"**; i.e., punishment in hell. Three verses later, in verse 10, he again warns of a **"painful chastisement" (Koran, *Shakir*)**. Thirteen verses later he writes of **"the fire whose fuel is men . . . [it is] prepared for the unbelievers" (v. 23)**.

This in turn is echoed in verse 39 where infidels are described as **"inmates of the fire; and there they shall abide forever."** Still another warning of damnation comes up in verse 48. Verse 81 again warns that evildoers **"shall be inmates of the fire, there shall they abide forever."** Four verses later he writes of **"grievous punishment on the day of resurrection" (v. 79)**, followed in verse 86 by **"Their punishment shall not be mitigated,"** and a grim warning of **"God's curse"** falling upon infidels **(v. 89)**!

Verse 90 includes the phrase **"wrath upon wrath"** resulting in **"a disgraceful punishment for unbelievers" (*Shakir*)**. Verse

96 warns of God's **"scourge,"** followed two verses later with the threat: **"God is the enemy of the unbelievers" (v. 98)**.

A reasonable reader expects Mohammed to ease eventually from such avid exploitation of his hell theme. Instead, he keeps warming to it. Of the 286 verses (277 in Rodwell) in chapter 2, 1 out of every 9.5 threatens both non-Muslims and disobedient Muslims with utter damnation.

Even in subsequent chapters, Mohammed addresses scarcely any topic without constantly interrupting himself to warn his readers about hell. Chapter 3, with 200 verses, warns of hellfire in 1 out of 7.4 verses! The 176 verses in chapter 4 follow the same course—1 out of every 7.2 verses harp on hell. Chapter 5, with 120 verses, averages 1 flame-throwing threat in every 8 verses.

Does Mohammed ever leave the subject of hell alone long enough to render even 100 average-length verses without a single hell-threat? He does not.

In the Koran there is 1 threat of hell in every 7.9 verses!

Rodwell's English translation of the Koran counts 6,151 verses in its 114 chapters. Throughout, Mohammed hurls 783 threats of hellfire, wrath, eternal judgment and perdition against the by then well-singed mind of any reader who keeps reading to the end of his Koran.

That is 1 threat of hell in every 7.9 verses! (Longer verses with two or three warnings each are counted once.)

Granted, the Bible also warns against hell, but not with a frequency that shows writers obsessing on the subject. According to *New Strong's Exhaustive Concordance of the Bible* "hell" is mentioned 31 times in the Old Testament—once for every 774 verses.[3] Among the New Testament's 7,992 verses, "hell" and the nouns "perdition" and "fire" (when "fire" means "hell," not "zeal" or "revival") occur 74 times.[4] That is once for every 120 verses.

Some of Mohammed's hell-threats target only those who disobey God. Read further and the basis for damnation widens. Anyone who rejects his claim to be a prophet or questions the divine inspiration of the Koran is also doomed to eternal flame. Anyone who refuses to go to battle for Islam or retreats from a battle for Islam draws down the same threat (see Koran 8:16 and 9:49).

It is easy for us as non-Muslims to suggest that Muslims should ignore Mohammed's hell-threats—and his 109 war verses, too—and just contemplate *nice* verses in the Koran. For a Muslim, it is not that simple. Islam does not countenance accepting part of the Koran and disdaining the rest. Islamic authorities insist that all of the Koran is God's word settled in heaven from eternity past—abrogations, hell-threats and war verses included. Thus the Koran itself is a de facto crowbar radical Muslims can use to leverage moderate Muslims away from moderation toward radicalism. That is why the non-Muslim world—in its own defense—absolutely must take on the task of rebutting the Koran. It has always merited rebuttal. Now it is time for us to get on with the task no matter how much we would rather be doing something else.

If a modern author submitted anything like the Koran to a publisher, it would be rejected as a radical cult handbook designed to manipulate followers and intimidate detractors with terror. Mohammed's heavy-handed penchant for threatening almost everyone with hellfire may explain why many moderate Muslims simply do not read the Koran. Better to be guilty of not reading the foundation of one's faith than to read it and be frightened by its incessant hell-threats into accepting such radical harangues as normative!

Worse yet, for a devout Muslim to read the Koran and be disappointed—even outraged—by the many moral and stylistic flaws perforating it is a dire spiritual crisis. Doubting the Koran is punishable as apostasy in this life, with eternal suffering in hell (see Koran 2:39; 2:85 and 3:106).

Bear in mind that Mohammed's hundreds of repetitions on hell braid into repetitions of his other favorite themes as well.

Even readers who grant the divine origin of the Koran *a priori*—if accustomed to less repetitive literary styles—find it difficult to continue reading again and again what they have already read again and again. Several readers of the Koran have told me they struggled even to finish the first two chapters.

How many sensitive readers—Muslim or otherwise—have simply had to stop reading because they were frightened? Recurring descriptions of people forced to drink scalding water and writhing in hellfire till their skin blisters off, only to have their skin *healed* to be seared off again and again forever, may indeed cause nightmares.

Other themes Mohammed repeats ad nauseum include:

Approximately 100 times Mohammed quotes his God as confirming that he **"sent down this book** [Koran]**" (Koran 16:46; 21:10)** for guidance and as a warning. Again and again he admonishes mockers (and there were many) that their chiding echoes that which dozens of earlier prophets endured. Mohammed's logic: *Prophets warned and were mocked. I warn and am mocked. Ergo, I must be a prophet.* Could a man inspired by God be guilty of such flawed reasoning?

In earlier days, Mohammed must have spent time listening as Jews in Mecca (and perhaps in Medina, at least until his hostility erupted against them) narrated stories from the Old Testament in Arabic. From time to time, however, Jewish storytellers switched from Old Testament Scripture to Jewish fables, traditions and legends. Mohammed, as I have already pointed out in chapter 2, apparently did not know the difference.

Eager to demonstrate that God was confirming the Old Testament through his Koran, Mohammed narrated Jewish stories he had heard. Alas, in doing so, he unwittingly mixed fable and tradition with Scripture. While Jewish people traditionally draw heavily upon the writings of their rabbis, they always carefully delineate between man-said and God-given words.

In addition to the God-lifting-up-Mount-Sinai-to-pummel-Israel legend, another Jewish fable posited that God—when he created Adam—commanded every angel in heaven to prostrate himself before Adam, a mere man. Every angel did so except Satan. A thoughtful reader will think, *Aha! God was testing the angels, and Satan—this being prior to his fall—was the only angel who passed the test by saying, "I worship God alone!"*

But no—in Mohammed's mind, Satan's refusal to prostrate himself before Adam is why God expelled Satan from heaven. Thinking he was confirming another piece of inspired revelation from the Old Testament, Mohammed chose to canonize that bit of uninspired fluff in seven different chapters of the Koran.

That is equivalent to an author claiming in seven different chapters of a modern book that Santa Claus, the elves and Santa's reindeer are described in the Bible.

In another Jewish tradition, Abraham rebuked his father, Terah (Mohammed called him Azar), for worshiping idols. Mohammed—placing that old traditional Jewish story on a level with Scripture—recited it monotonously not only in chapter 6, verses 74-87, but again in chapters 9, 19, 21, 37 and 43!

Indeed, some biblical narratives are repeated in the Old Testament books of 1 Samuel and 2 Samuel, 1 Kings and 2 Kings and 1 Chronicles and 2 Chronicles, and in the four New

Testament Gospels, but only when *different narrators* give their versions for multiple witness verification. What was the point of *the same* narrator—Mohammed—reciting one story six times? Apparently someone wanted to fill more space, to give the Koran respectable bulk. Repetition of content was the only way to puff the Koran, given Mohammed's lack of a sufficient pool of varied material.

Actually Mohammed retells aspects of Abraham's story—with biblical and legendary content intertwined—in 24 of the Koran's first 87 chapters. That is 1 retelling in every 3.6 chapters.

As I noted in chapter 2, among Mohammed's other all-time favorite space-fillers is the saga of Moses and the pharaoh. In the Koran's first 89 chapters, Mohammed retells elements of Moses'

The story of the Passover lamb is omitted in all 27 tellings of the Moses-and-the-pharaoh epic.

confrontation with the pharaoh 27 times. That is 1 retelling in every 3.3 chapters. Seven of the 27 retellings contain quite detailed renditions of the Moses-and-the-pharaoh epic.

Strangely, as we have already learned, the story of the Passover lamb is omitted in all 27 tellings. It is absent even though most people inhabiting Mecca and Medina—pagans included—knew that Jews everywhere celebrate the Passover every year. Perhaps it was also known to many in Mecca that Christians identify Judaism's Passover lamb as a foreshadowing of Jesus. Furthermore, Mohammed was no stranger to Christians—including his first wife's cousin, Wareka.

Why would Mohammed delete such an integral component in 27 accounts of the same story? Could it be that Mohammed— determined to deny that Jesus died as the atoning *"Lamb of God, who takes away the sin of the world"* (John 1:29)—deliberately avoided even an Old Testament foreshadowing of Christ as atoner? Whatever the reason, Mohammed still claimed at least a dozen times that he was confirming the Christian evangel as well as the Jewish Scriptures (see Koran 2:97,101).

Expert at gutting essentials, Mohammed was equally adept at jumbling together and confusing bits and pieces of various Bible stories. In verse 28:38 and again in verses 40:36-37, Mohammed's pharaoh in the time of Moses in Egypt commands Haman (a Persian in the book of Esther) to build a tower of bricks as a means of access to the heavens—an idea lifted from the Sumerians' firing of bricks to build the tower of Babel, as mentioned in Genesis 11:4.

Again, all seven of the Koran translations I examined agree that Mohammed describes God as **"drowning pharaoh and all those with him" (17:103; 26:66)** in the sea. And yet, in 10:92 and 10:94 seven translators have God, speaking through Mohammed, claiming that the pharaoh did *not* drown. Because he repented and pleaded for mercy while drowning, God spared the pharaoh at the last moment. M. M. Ali has God saying: **"We will save you in your body" (Koran 10:92)**.

Three translators have **"We shall today save your body,"** trying to avoid a betraying contradiction. Surely God—if *he* inspired the Koran—would know better than to contradict himself regarding the pharaoh's fate.

Mohammed kept on recycling other apocalyptic stories as well. He references Noah, hero of the biblical flood account, in 28 of the Koran's first 71 chapters—that is once in every 2.5 chapters. The story of Lot and the destruction of his people— even though Lot was not a native, but a foreigner, in Sodom and

Gomorrah—comes up in 14 chapters. Tales of legendary Arab cities and heroes Ad, Thamud, Shu'aib and Salih are also repeated about a half-dozen times each.

Mohammed's apocalyptic recitations stress a point: God destroys people who reject divine warnings delivered by prophets. Honoring himself as a prophet, Mohammed warned that God would likewise doom every contemporary who rejected *his* warnings. Yet in 15 verses of the Koran, Mohammed added something to earlier warnings. Where some verses originally only called upon people to obey God, Mohammed began to add, **"Obey God and his Apostle" (Koran 3:32)**.

Ten of Mohammed's apocalyptic stories end with the same command: **"Roam the earth and see what was the end of those who [rejected a prophet's warning]" (Koran 27:69** and others**)**.

Twenty-eight times in his first 79 chapters, Mohammed described his God-given mission as limited to one task: to be **"a warner only" (Koran 11:12; 13:7** and others**)**. Yet time after time Mohammed overstepped that supposedly God-given limitation. Every time he ordered an assassination or took up arms against infidels in Mecca or Jews in Medina, Mohammed violated God's **"warner only"** bind. Did he really think no one would notice?

If every statement or story that is repeated in the Koran were given *only once*, the entire Koran would slim down to approximately 40 percent of its published length.

Too Many Pronouns, Too Few Nouns

Still another idiosyncrasy of Mohammed's literary style devastates any hope that his Koran may be considered a literary classic: *Mohammed replaces several hundred very-needed nouns with frustratingly ambiguous pronouns.*

Every storyteller knows that readers need *nouns* primarily and pronouns only secondarily to help them differentiate persons, things and places. This is true in every culture, even those in the Middle East. The Bible, for example, invariably reveals—if not the personal names of persons in its narratives—at least their titles, offices or relationships. Readers of the Bible always know if individuals or groups in a story are Jews, Syrians, Egyptians, Canaanites, Moabites, Babylonians or whatever.

The Koran, on the other hand, omits important nouns *hundreds of times*.

Even N. J. Dawood, translator of one of the versions of the Koran I consulted in preparing for this book and the version I quote most often, acknowledges that "the Koran contains many statements which, if not recognized as altogether obscure, lend themselves to more than one interpretation. I have taken pains to reproduce these ambiguities wherever they occur, and have provided explanatory footnotes in order to avoid turning the text [itself] into an interpretation rather than a translation."[5]

Apparently Islam's Allah had no heavenly copy editor to edit all such ambiguities out of his eternally preexisting Koran before he gave it to Gabriel to give to Mohammed to give to mankind.

As an example, in 8:18, Mohammed dictated and a scribe wrote: **"If you were seeking a judgment, now has a judgment come to you. If you desist, it will be best for you" (Koran)**.

Mohammed used the pronoun "you" four times in two sentences. *Who* was he addressing? *What* was the judgment about? *Who* should desist from *what*? Mohammed does not specify answers to any of these questions anywhere, not even in the context of the verse.

Some translators of the Koran replace at least some of Mohammed's excess of pronouns with the nouns they think we would find if we could read the mind of a man who died nearly 1,400 years ago. Other translators just leave us at risk for pronoun poisoning.

A few, such as Dawood, footnote some of Mohammed's numerous ambiguous pronouns, explaining who or what they *think* he meant. Mohammed has cost countless scholars thousands of hours researching thousands of hadithic traditions for clues as to just who or what he was referring.

Indeed—Mohammed's monsoon of pronouns in the Koran draws sighs even from some Muslims. His rambling, repetitive prose affects some of them like chloroform, too. Mohammed's dearth of nouns in the Koran is the main thing that made the hadiths—filled as they are with noun-rich testimony from contemporaries of Mohammed—ever more important. The hadiths explain hundreds of pronoun-heavy verses in the Koran, only in a much better style. But it is the Koran, not the hadiths, that is supposed to be inspired!

Note how Rodwell daringly guesses at Mohammed's missing nouns in 8:18 (quoted above) by adding italicized nouns: **"O *Meccans!* If ye desired a decision, now hath a decision come to you. It will be better for you if ye give over *the struggle*"** **(Koran)**. Clearer indeed!

Defense 5: Violence Against Jews and Other Non-Muslims Was Justifiable at Islam's Beginning, but No One Need Fear Muslim Violence Now

Muslim apologists frequently aver that the battles Mohammed and his immediate successors fought against Jews and others were legitimate acts of self-defense. This claim deceives many who are unfamiliar with the Koran or the history of its origin. No Caesar Augustus or King George was taxing the Arabs in Mohammed's day. Mohammed was no George Washington leading freedom fighters against tyranny. Mecca and Medina were independent city-states. Each was led by a consensus of its leading men—a somewhat democratic rule measured by standards of the time. Mohammed was the one seeking to impose a professedly theocratic despotism upon a population troubled by little more than occasional violent interclan rivalry and the crime that is always present to some degree even in well-governed societies.

John L. Esposito, professor of Islamic Studies at Georgetown University, is perhaps the most erudite apologist for Islam in history. His book *Islam: The Straight Path* is used as a text in hundreds of college-level courses on Islam across America and throughout the English-speaking world.[6] He is also the editor of the *Oxford*

> ## Mohammed was no George Washington leading freedom fighters against tyranny.

Encyclopedia of the Modern Islamic World. How, then, does *he* justify Mohammed's violence against Meccans and Jews? He writes: "Muhammed's use of warfare in general was alien neither to Arab custom nor to that of the Hebrew prophets. Both believed that God had sanctioned battle with the enemies of the Lord."[7] Esposito follows that statement with references to Moses, Joshua and others battling Israel's enemies. These references are intended to assure us that Mohammed, by marauding caravans, butchering poets and enslaving or exiling Jews, was placing himself firmly in the tradition of the Hebrew prophets.

Professor Esposito is foisting an incredible anachronism. By Mohammed's day, 1,500 years had passed since any Hebrew prophet was described in the Old Testament as using a sword in the service of God. Neither Isaiah, Jeremiah, Ezekiel, Daniel, Micah, Amos, Malachi nor any other later Hebrew prophet is described as using the sword or prescribing its use. In addition, Talmudic writings tended to affirm the Jews of Mohammed's day to live well above the standards of Joshua's or Solomon's times.

New Testament writings also—especially in times when Christians were permitted eyes-on access to them—tended to lift Christians well above standards that endorsed marauding, killing and enslavement. Politically as well, the Jews that Mohammed encountered in Arabia had long before left the Bronze Age government of Joshua's day far behind. Yet Mohammed, ever so anachronistically, was time-lapsing back to something even more primitive—all with Professor Esposito's approval! Professor Esposito is essentially admitting that Mohammed launched Islam as a 1,600-year *throwback!* One would expect something inspired by God in the A.D. 600s to bring us a step upward to an even higher ethical standard. Instead, as Esposito unwittingly admits, Islam began as an unabashed reversion to primitivism.

Esposito declares: "After each major battle [that Muslims fought against Meccans] one of the Jewish tribes [in Medina] was accused and punished. . . . Muslim perception of distrust, intrigue and rejection on the part of the Jews led first to exile and later to warfare."[8]

The only evidence Esposito offers to support the charge that Jews in Medina were thus accused is one extremely vague quote from the Koran. He claims, "The Quran accuses the Jewish tribes of regularly breaking . . . pacts [sic. There was only one, the so-called Consitution of Medina]."[9] Esposito then quotes: **"Why is it that whenever they make pacts, a group among them casts it aside unilaterally" (Koran 2:100).**[10]

Could this be Esposito's own wording of 2:100? I find no other version of the Koran with anything like his addition of the word "unilaterally." Curiously, Mohammed's "it," a singular pronoun in the quote, has "pacts," a plural noun, as its referent. Most important, 2:100 only accuses "a group among them," rather than *all* of whoever Mohammed meant by "them," of breaking pacts (or is it a pact?). Esposito, in a most unscholarly way, amplifies Mohammed's complaint against "a group among" the Jews into a complaint against "the Jewish tribes" in their entirety. So—if it was only "a group among" the Jews that broke a pact, why could not Mohammed—the man everyone trusted to be an arbiter—simply negotiate with the majority of the Jews to rein in the rebels and keep the peace?

The plain truth is, neither Mohammed nor Esposito nor any other Muslim apologist offers a single piece of real evidence to justify Mohammed's wantonly brutal exiling, slaughtering and enslaving of Jews in Medina. It was a criminal atrocity. Mohammed merited being tried, convicted and either incarcerated or executed for a maniacal crime.

One would think a scholar of Esposito's erudition would be able to add at least one quote from the many volumes of hadithic literature to back up his one frail quote from the Koran. Alas, he marshals not even one bit of evidence from early Muslim hadithic sources to show that Muslims actually did accuse Jews of collaborating with Mecca prior to each of the three Muslim attacks against Jews in Medina—let alone that Muslims possessed *evidence* for any such accusations, even if we grant that accusations were made!

The truly revealing words in Esposito's sentence quoted above are "distrust . . . and rejection on the part of the Jews." *That* was the crux of the matter. The Jews, for abundant valid reasons, did not trust Mohammed. The Jews, for equally abundant valid reasons, rejected Mohammed's claim of prophethood. It was for *that* cause that he exiled, slaughtered and enslaved them.

I'm guessing that a pro-Muslim bias in Professor Esposito wanted to obscure the facts, but the scholar in him would not be denied and let the truth slip out. Yet in the same paragraph, Esposito makes still another stab at the impossible task of acquitting Mohammed from being charged as a genocidal murderer. Esposito pleads: "It is important to note that the motivation for such actions [i.e., the exiling, killing and enslavement of the Jews in Medina] was political rather than . . . theological."[11]

This constitutes an admission that if Mohammed's motivation *was* theological, he would have been reprehensible. From the professor's lack of evidence to the contrary and from his own words quoted above, it is clear that Mohammed's primary motivation was to retaliate against the Jews for rejecting his claim of prophethood. Hence Mohammed's motivation *was* theological. Hence Mohammed *is* reprehensible in historical perspective.

That is not to say that Mohammed had no secondary motivation as well. Lust for the lovely Jewish woman Rayhana and desire to plunder Jewish homes, land, date palm orchards and businesses no doubt added brute zeal to Mohammed's theological miff. Nor must we perceive the Jews as entirely blameless. Even people with faults of their own still had every right to defend themselves against the enslavements, assassinations and caravan plundering that had already become Mohammed's trademark.

Consider again the case of the Jewish clans that Mohammed evicted from their homes and businesses in Medina and the third clan he subjected to slaughter and enslavement. None of the three opposed the decision of Medinan Arabs to invite Mohammed to the city as an arbiter for local disputes. Indeed, Medinan Jews accepted the so-called Constitution of Medina, which Mohammed established initially to facilitate greater order in the city. Muslim scholar Ibn Ishaq, quoted by Ibn Warraq, describes that constitution as

> A treaty and covenant with the Jews, establishing them in their religion and possessions, and assigning to them rights and duties.[12]

Did the Jews in Medina shift from trust to hostility toward Mohammed soon after he arrived from Mecca? Apparently not, otherwise all three major clans would surely have united against him when he violated his own constitution by attacking the first Jewish clan. The failure of all three clans to exploit the advantage of fighting him collectively shows them to be a peace-preferring people, a group not accustomed to plotting military stratagems. The two remaining clans seem to have still hoped for peaceful coexistence with Mohammed even after he brutally evicted the first Jewish community.

Muslims have no basis to portray Mohammed's treachery and violence against Medinan Jews as self-defense.

There is also another matter. If the Jews were planning or even fearing conflict with the Muslims, surely they would have stored up much extra food and water in their respective fortresses in preparation for a possible long siege. Instead, Muslim records show that each time the Muslims attacked, the Jews did not have resources for a long siege and were forced to surrender within a few days! That is a very curious lack of preparedness for people with hostile intent.

And if Medinan Jews later began to hope for—and even request—help from Mecca to remove this arbitrator-turned-traitor from their own hometown, they were well within their rights!

Muslims have no basis to portray Mohammed's treachery and violence against Medinan Jews as self-defense. Nor do they have grounds to insist that the Koran's 109 war verses (see appendix B) authorized Muslims to use violence *only* at Islam's beginning in Arabia, but not anywhere else, and certainly not today. I have already shown from Mohammed's own words that he intended the violence he personally precipitated to be exemplary for his followers as Islam expanded on its way to become what he hoped would be the world's only religion.

Here are two examples of contemporary Muslim apologists who try to oppose the perception of Islam as a religion that is not only born *in* violence, but also bred to *be* violent.

Dr. Hasan Hathout

A professedly moderate Muslim apologist who freely spreads *radically* unjustified claims for Islam is Dr. Hasan Hathout, a spokesman for the Los Angeles-based Islamic Center of Southern California. Dr. Laura Schlessinger's three-hour radio interview with Hathout was aired nationally on October 5, 2001.[13] The conversation very instructively reveals the subtle strategies of a skilled Islamic apologist.

Dr. Laura asked Hathout if it was indeed true that Islam was engaged in "an apocalyptic struggle against the West to create an Islamic world." Hathout knew that a truthful yes! would confirm suspicions and raise fears about Islam's goals in the West. He also knew that a no! response might cause him to be jeered as a coward by radical Muslims. So Hathout cleverly avoided the issue. "Laura," he answered, "I have learned not to believe everything I read."

Dr. Laura and her listeners may have mistaken that for a no, but it was not a denial; it was a sidestep.

Dr. Laura very much needed to say, "Dr. Hathout, you have not answered my question." But, like many other Western media personalities trying to interview Muslim apologists, she let herself be distracted from her goal by an evasive answer.

Later she asked Hathout if it was true that Muslim suicide bombers each expect to be rewarded for their sacrifice by being given a bevy of 72 lovely virgins with whom they can have sex forever in paradise. A laughing Hathout replied, "That is exotic folklore!"

If Dr. Laura had done a little more homework before inviting a Muslim to be interviewed, she could have power pointed and read aloud for Hathout and her listening audience the five passages in the Koran that promise supplies of heavenly virgins for the pleasure of Muslim men in paradise. Then she could have said, "So, then, you believe the Koran contains 'exotic folklore'?"

That research would also have shown her that the Koran does not mention the number 72. But since she included the number in her question, she gave Hathout an opportunity to object to that one erroneous detail, leaving Dr. Laura and her audience to think he meant that the entire idea of virgins in paradise was exotic folklore. *That basic idea*, he clearly knew, is not at all regarded as exotic folklore. It *is found in* five passages in the Koran.

Hathout added, "To kill oneself is forbidden in Islam," even though verse 2:207 in Dawood's translation comes close to describing suicide. The passage declares: **"There are those who would give away their lives in order to find favor with God."** Ahmed Ali renders the key phrase in the same verse with a translation in the singular case: **"He will sell his soul."** There is a major difference between seeking a violent death to gain merit—in the radical Muslim sense—and being willing to lay down one's life when obedience to God or love for another person renders the choice unavoidable—which is the New Testament concept.

When Dr. Laura quoted a series of five or six war verses, Hathout declared in response to each one that the call for violence was "temporary, meant only for that time and situation."

That was where Dr. Laura needed to become attorney Schlessinger, asking, "Exactly what was it about *that* time and situation that made violence justifiable *then*?" Once Hathout cited some crisis that Muslims were immersed in back then, she could ask, "Doesn't that mean that any Muslim today who finds himself in a situation *just like that one* will be also justified in seeking to resolve the situation with violence?"

If Hathout said, "No, not today," she could have asked, "Quote the verse in the Koran that assures all of us non-Muslims today that Muslims *since then* are forbidden ever to use violence against 'people of the book' the way Mohammed authorized the first Muslims to do." Hathout would have then found himself in an increasingly difficult situation.

Instead, as the interview progressed, Hathout declared that "the U.S. Constitution is the essence of true Islam." An obvious rejoinder could be, "Then why is there not one single true democracy among the 55 nations of the Muslim world?"

An inadequately informed Western interviewer enables an Islamic propagandist to promote Islam.

When a caller posed a similar question, Hathout replied that Islam has not yet been truly manifested in any Muslim country because they "are all under dictatorships." One must ask—Why then is Iran, ruled by Muslim clerics, also a dictatorship? And— If Islam is such a marvelous spiritual *and political* force on Earth, why hasn't it succeeded in replacing *at least one* dictatorship with a government that guarantees human rights?

Oddly there is a certain truth to Hathout's declaration that the U.S. Constitution has something in common with Islam. One amendment to the U.S. Constitution guarantees a woman's right to vote, but there is *nothing* in the Constitution that guarantees a married woman's right, barring death or divorce, to be her husband's *sole spouse*. Islam lets a man have *four* spouses. So yes, in that instance, the U.S. Constitution is "the essence of Islam." But in myriad other ways, it is the antithesis of Islam.

So it happens again and again. An inadequately informed Western interviewer enables an Islamic propagandist to promote Islam widely and for free.

Dr. Kaled Abou El Fadl

Occasionally a moderate Muslim speaks out against radical forms of Islam, but rarely if ever at the cost of denying the utter integrity and divine inspiration of the Koran. For example, the *Los Angeles Times* on January 2, 2002, carried a front-page tribute to Khaled Abou El Fadl, a Muslim professor—not of Islam, but of law—at UCLA, for taking radical fellow Muslims to task for "intolerant puritanism."[14]

Abou El Fadl's diatribes by e-mail, in lectures and in books are enraging radical Muslims all the way from Los Angeles to Saudi Arabia. He has received so many death threats that he is having a security system installed around his home.

Perusing Teresa Watanabe's *Times* report, I note that Abou El Fadl's strategy is to search out obscure but moderate hadiths to counteract the influence of the much better known and far more commonly quoted war verses in the Koran and in radical hadiths. By this means he seeks to persuade Muslims to favor tolerance and moderation.

Clearly Abou El Fadl despairs of finding *within the Koran itself* the means to offset the effect of the Koran's own war verses and the corresponding blood spatter in radical hadiths. The fact that a man who knows Islam so well does not quote the Koran when arguing *with Muslims* on behalf of moderation is revealing. You can do that for apologetic purposes with unapprised non-Muslims, but arguing for moderation with well-informed Muslims requires you to lay the Koran to one side and resort to obscure hadiths. Informed Muslims *know* that the Koran does not advocate moderation!

There is not a single shred of evidence in Watanabe's article that Abou El Fadl *ever* discredits or rejects anything Mohammed said *in the Koran*. That is why we should take no encouragement at all from Abou El Fadl's efforts, well-intentioned as they no doubt are. Using rationalizations based on obscure hadiths to try to counter the Koran while still accrediting the Koran itself is like trying to slow down a hurricane by asking moths to beat their wings against the wind.

Defense 6: Blame Jews and Christians, not Mohammed, for the Disparities That Exist Between Biblical Stories and Mohammed's Revisions of the Same

Muslim apologists insist that Jews and Christians tampered with the original text of their respective Scriptures, requiring God through Mohammed to restore both the Old and New Testaments back to their original copy via the Koran.[15] This onerous tenet obligates Muslim mullahs to teach in Islamic mosques that of course there never was, for example, a Passover event in the original Exodus story. Jews just added that capriciously. Nor was there ever a Gideon who selected 300 warriors. Someone knew it was King Saul but wrote Gideon's name in for mischief.

This is equivalent to a man buying the house next door and then declaring that someone tampered with the title to your house and the house of the neighbor on the other side, but rejoice! He has corrected the tampering and now all three houses belong to him! Bad neighbor indeed! In the real world, a court of law would stop his fraud, but in the unreal world of Islamic theologizing there is nothing like a court of appeal for two defrauded biblical testaments. Islam arrogantly flaunts this tenet—however baseless—because that's what it takes to white-wash Mohammed and the Koran and serve its own interests.

Consider that Jesus, the apostles and Christians down through the centuries have not revised a single word of the Old

Testament apart from—in more recent times—comparing old texts newly found. Jewish and Christian scholars have frequent consultations. But Muslim scholars see no need to compare ancient texts. They already know without asking.

Consider also that God, if he were really speaking through Mohammed, could have—indeed should have, if it was so—declared that he could not confirm the Jewish and Christian Scriptures because they were corrupted. Instead, several dozen times, Mohammed declares that the Jewish and Christian Scriptures are *confirmed*—not *corrected*—by his Koran. Surely

---

Mohammed declares that the Jewish and Christian Scriptures are *confirmed*— not *corrected*—by his Koran.

Allah would not confirm anything that had been corrupted. The simple fact is that Mohammed himself did not regard the Old and New Testaments as corrupted. Muslim apologists are actually correcting Mohammed's misperception concerning them.

As I have already noted, the Koran criticizes Jews for disbelieving or disobeying the Old Testament and for copying bits of it to sell to pagan Arabs for **"a paltry price" (Koran 2:38)**, but *not for corrupting the actual text.*

If only Mohammed had thought of the modern Muslim apologist's way of countering Jewish disapproval of his distortions of the Old Testament, perhaps he would not have felt compelled to evict, kill or enslave them for criticizing him. But once Jews in Medina were evicted, killed, enslaved, converted or terrorized into sullen silence no one was left to reprimand Mohammed for his rambling, far-fetched mistellings of Old Testament stories.

Only 200 years later did Muslim scholars finally begin to read the Old Testament itself in Hebrew, in the Greek Septuagint or in Jerome's Vulgate translation in Latin. Only then did Muslim scholars confront a mass of evidence that their so-called prophet had canonized a very uninspired jumble of erroneous borrowings from the Old Testament, coupled with his own private imaginings. Forced to concede Mohammed's fraud or blame the Jews for tampering with Scripture, Muslim scholars very unobjectively chose the second option.

In the entire history of textual criticism there is no evidence that Old Testament texts ever matched Mohammed's Koranic variances. If such evidence were ever found, Muslim apologists would be exploiting it. As it is, they are silent on the matter.

Defense 7: God Gave Isaac's Descendants—the Jews— a Revelation in Hebrew. Would He Not Also Give Isaac's Half-Brother, Ishmael, a Revelation in Arabic for His Descendants?

Seventh-century Arab polytheists, observing the greater literary, commercial and cultural advancements of neighboring monotheists, i.e., Jews and Christians in the Roman Empire, began to associate monotheism with progress. This—combined with a growing sense of their own relative backwardness—stirred within the Arab ethos a general longing for a better-late-than-never cultural and religious sprint to try to match the perceived refinements of Jews and Christians.

Mohammed skillfully offered Arabs three things: himself as a prophet, his Koran as scripture and his Allah-centered monotheism as basis for a grand-scale let's-get-equal-with-Jews-and-Christians effort. He emphasized Arab descendancy from Abraham via Ishmael to legitimize his offering. Once again, however, he altered the very Old Testament revelation he constantly professed to affirm.

In Genesis 17:18, Abraham pleaded with God, saying, *"If only Ishmael might live under your blessing."* God replied, *"As for Ishmael, I have heard you: I will surely bless him . . . will make him into a great nation. But my covenant I will establish with Isaac, whom Sarah will bear to you"* (Genesis 17:20-21).

God again affirmed Isaac as the primary heir, saying: *"It is through Isaac that your offspring will be reckoned. I will make [Ishmael] into a nation also, because he is your offspring"* (Genesis 21:12-13).

Just as God later favored Jacob, the younger sibling, above Esau, the firstborn, so God in Abraham's day promised Ishmael, the elder half brother, an impressive descendancy, but selected second-born Isaac as scion of God's covenant with Abraham.

Supremacist philosophy remained one of Islam's primary policy bases throughout the Middle Ages and has renewed potency today.

Perhaps unaware of the above divine decision, recorded nearly 2,600 years earlier, Mohammed—claiming descendancy from Isaac's half brother Ishmael—initially attempted to establish Islam as a *fraternal* religion alongside Judaism (and to a lesser extent alongside Christianity). But—failing to show the signs of a true prophet among Jews in Medina—he essentially undermined his own plan A.

Then, slaughtering some Jews in Medina—dispossessing and enslaving others—Mohammed in effect resorted to a de facto plan B. Islam was no longer fraternal to Judaism; it became fratricidal instead.

Chronologically, later chapters of the Koran (their order in the Koran itself is not chronological) and numerous hadiths show Mohammed revoking his earlier egalitarianism vis-à-vis Judaism and Christianity. He imbued Islam laterally with a strongly supremacist attitude toward the two older monotheisms. Verse 61:9 is a prime example: **"Make [Islam] victorious over every other religion" (Koran)**. Supremacist philosophy remained one of Islam's primary policy bases throughout the Middle Ages and has renewed potency today.

Supremacism in the Koran, launched as it was with bloodshed, treachery and enslavement, differs vastly from what some might call supremacism in the New Testament. Jesus commanded us to be *"the salt of the earth"* and *"the light of the world"* (Matthew 5:13-14). He added, *"Let your light shine before men, that they may see your good deeds and praise your Father in heaven"* (Matthew 5:15). Jesus taught us to pray, *"Our Father in heaven, hallowed be your name, your kingdom come, your will be done on earth as it is in heaven"* (Matthew 6:9-10).

If that is supremacism, then yes, the New Testament is supremely supremacist.

Notes

1. Muhammad Zafulla Khan, trans., *The Quran* (New York: Olive Branch Press, 1997), n.p.
2. Ibid.
3. *New Strong's Exhaustive Concordance of the Bible* (Iowa Falls, IA: World Bible Publishers), n.p.
4. Ibid.
5. N. J. Dawood, trans., *The Koran* (New York: Penguin Putnam, 1999), p. 5.
6. John L. Esposito, *Islam: The Straight Path*, 3rd ed. (New York: Oxford University Press, 1998), p. X; copyright 1998 by Oxford University Press, Inc. Used by permission.
7. Ibid., p. 15.
8. Ibid.
9. Ibid. (See chapter 2.)
10. Ibid., p. 15.
11. Ibid.
12. Ibn Warraq, *Why I Am Not a Muslim* (Amherst, NY: Prometheus Books, 1995), p. 92.

13. Hasan Hathout, interview by Laura Schlessinger, "Dr. Laura on the Radio," October 5, 2001, Premeire Radio Networks, quoted in Randall Price, *Unholy War* (Eugene, OR: Harvest House, 2001), pp. 211-214.

14. Teresa Watanabe, "Battling Islamic Puritans," *Los Angeles Times*, January 2, 2002, n.p.

15. Esposito, *Islam*, p. 12.

CHAPTER SEVEN

NON-MUSLIM ATTEMPTS TO DEFEND THE KORAN

On January 30, 2002, cable television network C-SPAN 2 aired a talk given by Karen Armstrong, a specialist in the history of various religions. She was speaking to an audience at the Egyptian embassy in Washington, D.C. Her topic: "Islam and the Other World Religions."

A HISTORIAN'S REPORT

Evidently impressed by the gentle treatment Armstrong gave Mohammed and the Koran in her recent book *Muhammed: A Biography of the Prophet*, Egyptian embassy officials invited her to speak, probably wanting her assistance in damage control for Islam after September 11, 2001.

I watched dumbfounded as Armstrong, without describing the actual appalling events, excused Mohammed's slaughter and enslavement of Medinan Jews as "a just defensive war."[1] I wondered, *Why does a noted historian so egregiously squander her reputation as an objectivist?*

If Armstrong had been present among the Jews in Medina, would she have advised them to acknowledge Mohammed as an Old Testament-confirming prophet when both they and she could see he was no such thing? It was not obvious at first that anyone's refusal to validate him would be construed by him as a capital offense. So even tipping Mohammed a pseudoaffirmation merely to survive his wrath for the moment would not have seemed necessary.

Next, Armstrong described Mohammed as "tolerant" because, after evicting two Jewish clans from their homes, beheading a bunch of men and enslaving everyone remaining in a third Jewish clan, he deigned to allow one or two smaller Jewish groups to stay in Medina.[2]

Armstrong failed to mention the mental state of any Jews who stayed in Medina after the so-called prophet's horrifying evictions and slaughterings of their compatriots. They were either traumatized into converting to Islam or shushed by sheer terror from voicing their utter disbelief in Mohammed.

In the skewed logic of a Karen Armstrong, an ounce of condescension by Mohammed outweighs a ton of atrocity. Armstrong merits both a rebuke and a rebuttal from every Jew and Jewish organization. Alas, modern Jews seem quite uninformed about the mass murders Mohammed perpetrated upon their people in Medina and later in other towns of Arabia as well.

Armstrong credited Mohammed for pluralism because at first he commanded Muslims to pray three times per day facing toward Jerusalem instead of Mecca. Other scholars regard that ploy as only one of several carrots on a stick Mohammed used to try to induce Jews to betray their own good sense by crediting him as a prophet. As soon as it was clear to Mohammed that he could not subvert them, he showed utter scorn for the Jews by ordering all Muslim prayer directed five times per day toward Mecca.

Attempting to explain Islam's al-Qaeda-type terrorism comfortingly, Armstrong first linked it with Jewish and Christian *fundamentalism* and then—as if vying for first prize in a sweeping generalization contest—declared that "all fundamentalists are motivated by *fear*."[3]

Ask any Jewish or Christian fundamentalist if he or she is motivated by fear and almost all will answer, "No! We believe in God, and we want His goodness and justice to prevail by good and just means." But of course, Armstrong knows fundamentalists better than they know themselves. Only people who share her views are capable of being motivated by *principle*. Religious conservatives can only react like cornered animals.

During a question-and-answer time after her talk, Armstrong fielded a question from the audience about the status of women under Islam. She smilingly affirmed Mohammed as "a man who truly enjoyed the presence of women!"[4]

Yes, indeed! He relished dozens of women, nine-year-old Aisha and female slaves among them, all submissively captive in his harem. Include also the Jewess, Rayhana, forced to submit to Mohammed, the murderer of her husband. How she must have loathed the so-called prophet's *enjoyment* of her on the same day her husband was murdered.

My eyebrows nearly bounced off the ceiling. Armstrong, a woman, was blithely endorsing not only Mohammed's ethnic purging of embattled Jews but even his self-serving polygamy and rapacious sexual abuse of numerous female slaves.

What about the slaying of poetess Asma bint Marwan among her babies? (See chapter 2.) What about Mohammed's endorsement—recorded in a hadith—of the prior Arab custom of female genital mutilation (FGM)?[5] (More on this later in this chapter.) One ruling from him would have abolished the cruel Arab practice. Instead, he gave approval, and hundreds of millions of women, not only Arab but also Persian, Egyptian, Syrian, Pakistani, Algerian, Malaysian and Indonesian, have had to endure genital disfigurement by the Arabs during the last 1,400 years.

Is that enjoyment of women or sadistic antifemale masochism?

Who better to endorse a pseudoprophet than a heavily compromised historian? Imagine the Egyptian embassy mass mailing copies of Armstrong's videotaped lecture to the four winds. Imagine Muslim apologists and organizations exploiting her as a barker for Islam in university classrooms and luncheons across the non-Muslim world. Thus has Karen Armstrong made herself a de facto disinformation agent for Islam. Surely she would not choose to see her world dominated by Islam. Yet she unwittingly caters to a force which, at its radical core, would tyrannize every non-Muslim, if it could.

I found a copy of Armstrong's *Muhammad*. I was eager to see if her book showed more objectivity than her lecture which was given, as it was, at a Muslim event. Alas, her book and lecture match! I was also eager to check her sources. Could there be, I wondered, a body of scholarly research drawing conclusions so drastically opposite of those of my four primary sources: Muir, Rodinson, Warraq and Bat Ye'or?

Armstrong—admitting she knew virtually nil about Islam until she decided to write books about it—makes no mention of

Muir nor of Warraq or Ye'or, whose books were published *after* hers but before her lecture tour. But she claims Maxime Rodinson as her main source.

Well, I too have a copy of Rodinson's work. Searching for it for a long time and in vain, finally I found a website featuring titles offered in 70,000 used-book stores. Only one—a shop in Eau Claire, Wisconsin—had Rodinson's tome. One quick telephone call and it was mine!

May the whole world know that Rodinson, like Muir before him and Ibn Warraq and Bat Ye'or after, criticizes Mohammed for murdering, enslaving and otherwise terrorizing thousands of innocent people. May the whole world know that Karen Armstrong misrepresents the conclusions of her own primary source.

Newsweek on the Bible and the Koran

Armstrong is not the only Western writer lullabying the Western world about Islam while the threat of Islamic supremacism looms. Kenneth L. Woodward (unlike *Robert* Woodward, famed for incisive investigative journalism with his exposé of the 1970s Watergate scandal and the subsequent toppling of the Nixon presidency) brings only a dull investigative edge to problems inherent in the Koran. In a February 11, 2002, cover piece for *Newsweek,* "The Bible and the Qur'an," Woodward seeks to reassure us about Islam. Woodward, *Newsweek*'s religion writer, first expresses pity for Arabs because until Mohammed "they had no sacred text to live by, like the Bible. . . . Above all, they had no prophet sent to them by God, as Jews and Christians could boast."[6]

How sad! For a start, the entire Bible clarifies that it, though given to the Jews, was not *just for them* (see Genesis 12:3; 18:18; 22:18; 26:4; 28:14; Isaiah 49:6; Luke 24:47; Acts 1:8; Revelation 5:9 and others).

As evidence that the Bible, as the first five biblical references in the preceding paragraph aver, was given to *"bless* [not terrorize] *all peoples on earth,"* not just the Jews who received it, consider that Christians—who are not one ethnic group, as are Jews and Arabs—received the entire Bible *from the Jews.* Every writer of the *New* Testament, with the possible exception of Luke, was a Jew.

What if Greeks, Latins, Gauls, Germanics and all the other ethnic groups who became Christians had refused to welcome the Bible, saying, "No! God must first give us each our own prophet and our own separate inspired book confirming the Bible in each of our languages, or we will not be monotheists!" (This is, incidentally, similar to Mormonism's baseless premise that the Bible—given in the Eastern Hemisphere—needed to be supplemented by the Book of Mormon for the Western Hemisphere.)

Multiplied similar demands, spreading across the planet, would by now have produced several thousand Mohammeds and several thousand Korans. Having a Koran for one's own ethos would be a worldwide hallmark of keeping up with the Jewish Joneses. Does *Newsweek's* Woodward really think the world needs *that*?

He admits: "The Qur'an does contain sporadic calls to violence, sprinkled throughout the text."[7] If they are truly *throughout* the text, are "sprinkled" and "sporadic" the best modifiers? He continues: "Though few in number, these aggressive verses have fired Muslim zealots in every age."[8] Apparently Muslim zealots, if only they had done a verse count, would have been moderates. Woodward is perhaps unaware that the Koran features at least 109 war verses, which can hardly be called "few." But at least he concedes that the impact of Mohammed's war verses far exceed the supposed infrequency of their appearance in the Koran. He implies that Koranic war verses carry "the force of divine commands."[9]

Yet Woodward advises us to ignore the out-of-proportion potency of the war verses and to be reassured by their purported relative infrequency. Poison in the soup is fine, supposedly, as long as the poison is only a small part of the contents.

By contrast, Woodward credits Jesus as the genuine peace inspirer one would expect the *Prince of Peace* to be. Woodward wrote: "Crusaders have fought with the cross on their shields [but] they did not—could not—cite words from Jesus to justify their slaughters."[10]

The Koran contains *nothing* comparable to Jesus' story of a Good Samaritan.

The article continues: "Compared with the few and much quoted verses that call for Jihad against the infidels, the Koran places far more emphasis on acts of justice, mercy and compassion."[11] As if Islam grants Muslims freedom to esteem part of the Koran and disdain the rest!

Acts of justice, mercy and compassion? *For whom?*

The answer Woodward's article overlooks is for anyone who is not an infidel; i.e., for *Muslims* only! When Muslims are friendly to non-Muslims, as many are, it is by their own choice. The Koran *commands* them to be that way only to their fellow Muslims. The Koran contains *nothing* comparable to Jesus' story of a Good Samaritan showing kindness to an outsider, a man of a different sect.

Woodward acknowledges that the Koran is full of repetitions, but ever so leniently reasons that this was because Arabs had to memorize the verses as dictated, and repetition aids memorization. But wait! If the repetitions *also* have to be memorized, doesn't that *add* rather massively to an already laborious memorization task? Wouldn't it be a much better aid to memorization just to *remove* all repetitions, leaving a mere third or so of the material that must be memorized?

Would learners add repetitions to the actual text to make it easier to memorize? Hardly. In any case, Muslims will reject Woodward's suggestion as violating the Koran's purported divine inspiration and scorn his suggestion that Muslims simply ignore the Koran's war verses and live by its peace verses.

Woodward also offers this shocking opinion: "In gospel terminology, the Qur'an corresponds to Christ himself, as the *logos*, or eternal word of the Father. In short, if Christ is the word made flesh, the Qur'an is the word made book."[12]

If that is true, Islam proclaims *the deification of a book!* But this presents a problem. Like Judaism and Christianity, Islam abhors idolatry. The essence of idolatry, however, is honoring a mere *thing* as deity. A book is a *thing*. Are we to view Islam as having come full circle, leading its followers from idolatry through monotheism *back to idolatry* by deifying a book? Moreover, isn't a deified Koran a second person in an Islamic godhead, contradicting Islam's insistence on the absolute oneness of deity?

If Robert Woodward was as indulgent with Nixon as Kenneth Woodward is with Mohammed, Nixon would have finished his presidency with colors flying. Moreover, *Newsweek*, like the *Los Angeles Times*, continues publishing article after article resembling a concerted public relations effort on behalf of Islam. Islam in America would be bankrupt if it had to pay for that much space in advertisements. Every article focuses on making Islam appear just as praiseworthy and viable as Judeo-Christianity.

Judeo-Christianity proclaims heaven as a place where those whom God redeems from this bedeviled world reunite with loved ones to worship their all-worthy God in purity, peace and joy forever. Along comes *Newsweek* reporter Lisa Miller to discuss—on the same level—Mohammed's callous misrepresentation of that same Judeo-Christian heaven as actually an enormous brothel in the sky. Mohammed's willingness to corrupt anything holy—even heaven—if doing so would lure ribald pagan men into his following is pathetically overlooked.[13]

Mohammed's twist on heaven is a mere 1,400 years old, so Miller attacks both the antiquity and clarity of Judeo-Christianity's understanding of heaven, as if doing so will cut Judeo-Christianity's older concept down to size, facilitating her on-the-same-level comparison of Islam's view. Miller ever so mistakenly declares that Jews, until 167 B.C., "had a largely inchoate idea of the hereafter [then] . . . Jewish leaders came up with a powerful incentive [to strengthen Jews against pagan influence]. 'Many of those who sleep in the dust of the earth shall awake, some to everlasting life, and some to shame and everlasting contempt,' says a passage from the Book of Daniel, written around 165 B.C. [sic]. This is the first full-blown reference to resurrection in the Bible."[14]

Job, a very long time before Daniel, wrote, *"After my skin has been destroyed, yet in my flesh I will see God,"* (Job 19:26). What is *half-blown* about that! David, centuries before Daniel, echoed, *"My body also will rest secure, because you will not abandon me to the grave, nor will you let your Holy One* [i.e., the Messiah] *see decay. . . . You will fill me with joy in your presence, with eternal pleasures at your right hand"* (Psalm 16:9-11). He ended his immortal Psalm 23 with *"I will dwell in the house of the* LORD *forever"* (v. 6).

What is *inchoate* about that!

Newsweek editors, your religion coverage is deteriorating before our very eyes.

"ISLAM: EMPIRE OF FAITH"

Next I must comment on a massive piece of disinformation for Islam aired repeatedly nationwide by the Public Broadcasting System (PBS) television. It is titled "Islam: Empire of Faith."

The very title warns that Islam is a religion that rejects the Western idea of separation of religion and state. Of course nothing in the content of PBS's three-hour presentation cautions Americans to be concerned about that ominously anti-Constitutional aspect of Islam.

I do not fault the narrator, Ben Kingsley, for his at times misleading comments. Kingsley was simply given a text to read and was paid to read it word for word. As for the contributing scholars, I know well how an editor may delete key lines, destroying the balance that a scholar intended to present. Still, some of the contributing scholars make statements that drastically misrepresent the facts about Islam.

"Islam: Empire of Faith" credits Islam for the marvelous spirit of inquiry that flourished in Muslim-controlled Middle Eastern regions during the Middle Ages. French historian Ernest Renan disagrees:

Science and philosophy flourished [under Islam] during the first half of the Middle Ages, but it was not by reason of Islam; it was in spite of Islam. Not a . . . philosopher or scholar escaped persecution. [For a while] the instinct of free inquiry and the rationalist tradition is kept alive, then intolerance and fanaticism win the day. It is true that the Christian Church also cast great difficulties in the way of science in the Middle Ages, but she did not strangle it outright as did the Muslim theology. To give Islam the credit [for] . . . so many illustrious thinkers who passed half their life [sic] in prison, in forced hiding, in disgrace, whose books were burned and whose writings almost suppressed by theological authority, is as if one were to ascribe to the Inquisition . . . a whole scientific development [which it tried to prevent].[15]

Clearly, it appears that someone had a strongly biased agenda in pushing this production. If Muslim sponsors are behind it, they deserve to have it backfire upon them. Here's why: Of course "Islam: Empire of Faith" must open with a *mild* bias—burping the obligatory compliment to the Koran as magnificent literature. A voice-over calls the Koran "more beautiful than the most exquisite Arab poetry"—which tells us Westerners absolutely nothing.[16]

Blatant bias quickly follows, bursting to the surface like a gigantic, multitentacled squid. "Islam: Empire of Faith" credits Mohammed with promulgating "a strong social justice message."[17] A scholar even claims that *that* was the basis of Mohammed's appeal to pagan Arab men. It even speaks of "his humbleness as a person."[18]

With that, we can see that "Islam: Empire of Faith" totally covers up the truth about Mohammed—that he was a marauder, stealing other people's property, having one innocent after another assassinated, ordering several hundred Jewish men beheaded, condemning captive women to spend their entire lives serving him and his followers as sex slaves, and selling hundreds of free Jewish boys into slavery.

"Islam: Empire of Faith" misleads again, describing the Battle of Badr as a concertedly anti-Muslim attack by Mecca against a small Muslim community that was fighting for survival. All significant Muslim sources admit that Mohammed himself provoked the battle by marauding Mecca's caravans. The Meccans were there *to defend an actual en route caravan* that Mohammed was preparing to attack.

"Islam: Empire of Faith" admits that in the Battle of Badr, "brother fought against brother, son against father,"[19] but fails to mention what I have already pointed out: that Mohammed taught his men not to hesitate while killing kinsmen, because Islam supercedes every other loyalty.[20]

One contributor mildly acknowledges what should be called Mohammed's obsession in the Koran for hurling hell-threats at almost everyone, saying that "there are references to the unjust going to the fire."[21] As I have already noted, 783 hell-threats is more than just references. It is a firestorm.

"Islam: Empire of Faith" makes much of Mohammed sparing Mecca from bloodshed when he finally conquered the city. Perhaps he felt a twinge of guilt for causing the slaughter of 49 of his fellow Meccan townsmen three years earlier at Badr and the beheading of hundreds of Jewish men at Medina. How much credit should one get for sparing the lives of people among whom he grew up?

"Islam: Empire of Faith" mocks medieval Christian Europe while praising Islamic civilization.

"Islam: Empire of Faith" then describes Islam's rapid spate of armed victories in Palestine, Syria, Iraq, North Africa and southern Spain. It makes no mention of Charles Martel's Franks defeating the Muslims at Tours—or the Habsburgs stopping a second major Muslim invasion at Vienna. To report that an Islamic army was ever defeated might embarrass Islam, perhaps.

The claim is made that Muslims built channels for running water in Tunisia "hundreds of years before anyone in Europe thought of running water."[22] Did not the Romans, many centuries earlier, build aqueducts to transport fresh water over hundreds of kilometers?

Several dozen times, "Islam: Empire of Faith" mocks medieval Christian Europe while praising Islamic civilization. The eventual collapse of Islam's golden age is blamed on the Mongol invasion. But medieval Europe's dark age is mentioned frequently with no acknowledgment that it was precipitated by an equally massive invasion by Huns, Goths, Visigoths and Vandals. Viewers are left to think Europe's dark age was due to Christianity's failure to uplift while Islam's golden age was the fruit of true faith.

Scholarship under Islam, especially in Baghdad, is credited with absorbing and processing both philosophical and mathematical concepts borrowed from Greece and India. No mention is made of Islam's persecution of scholars or its abject failure to borrow the single most important concept that Greece had to offer: democracy!

From its rise to its fall, Islamic civilization was always fractured. It never had one capital city, such as Rome. Sunnis and Shiites warred. Later Sunni factions and Shiite factions fought within their respective domains. "Islam: Empire of Faith" totally ignores Bat Ye'or's stereotype-shattering research, which reveals the Islamic empires—a more accurate term—as founded upon slavery and unjustly high taxes massively extorted from Christians, Jews, Zoroastrians and other minorities. Democracy and individual human rights were of no genuine concern to Muslim leaders then or now.

Christian Europe, recovering from its Hun-Goth-and-Vandal-imposed dark age, eventually caught up with and far surpassed the commendable accomplishments of Middle Eastern scholars in math and science. But just as important, it also assimilated the concept of democracy. Thus enabled, European nations went on to transform the world in even more significant ways than Islam could ever do with its focus on *submission, submission, submission under dictatorship.*

"Islam: Empire of Faith" describes Muslim rulers of the Ottoman phase as unable to trust their fellow Muslims who were found repeatedly to be far too prone to treacherous intrigue to be trusted as a sultan's personal bodyguards. So, as one Muslim contributor to "Islam: Empire of Faith" explains, "they *recruited* Christian children"[23] to be converted to Islam and

From its rise to its fall, Islamic civilization was *always* fractured. Democracy and individual human rights were of no concern to Muslim leaders then or now.

trained as the Sultan's special guards, called janissaries. The television program shows children aged five to eight as examples. How does one recruit children that young? Bat Ye'or's research reveals that there was no recruiting; there was only *kidnapping*. Sultans *stole* thousands of little Christian children from their anguished parents.

Yet "Islam: Empire of Faith" contributor, Esin Atil—a Muslim—smiles approvingly as she describes a Muslim policy that wracked thousands of Christian families with grief. It was the price they had to pay because Muslim rulers could not trust their fellow Muslims. What is *that* to be proud of?

The PBS special claims that the Muslim empire, in spite of all its fractures and disunity, was the largest that has ever been. The producers forget the fact that all of the world's treaty-linked, economically and politically cooperative English-speaking nations— Great Britain, the United States, Canada, Australia, New Zealand, Barbados, Jamaica, Kenya and others—can just as validly be viewed as a single politically and culturally interrelated "empire." It is much vaster and more populous than PBS's so-called Islamic empire ever was.

I could go on, but surely I have written enough to demonstrate that PBS's "Islam: Empire of Faith" is a disgraceful piece of Islamic disinformation.

Do Muslim apologists acknowledge the scholarship of my four main sources—Muir, Rodinson, Warraq and Ye'or? Perhaps the most widely read Muslim apologist today is Caesar E. Farah, Ph.D., at the University of Minnesota. In Farah's *Islam* he describes Sir William Muir's *Life of Mohammed* as "detailed and thorough, from original sources."[24] Farah also lists Rodinson's *Mohammed* as recommended reading. Rodinson quotes the same original sources as Muir. Ibn Warraq and Ye'or—published after 1994—are not mentioned by Farah, but they quote extensively from pre-1994 authors approved by Farah.

Notes

1. Karen Armstrong, "Speech by Karen Armstrong at the Egyptian Embassy 1/30: Islam and the Other World Religions" C-SPAN 2, January 30, 2002.
2. Ibid.
3. Ibid.
4. Ibid.
5. Jan Goodwin, *Price of Honor* (London: Warner Books, 1998), pp. 334-335; Jean Sasson, *Daughters of Arabia* (London: Bantam Books, 1998), pp. 198-201.
6. Kenneth L. Woodward, "The Bible and the Qur'an," *Newsweek* (February 11, 2002), p. 52.
7. Ibid.
8. Ibid.
9. Ibid., p. 53.
10. Ibid.
11. Ibid.
12. Ibid.
13. Lisa Miller, "Why We Need Heaven: Visions of Heaven and the Centuries-Old Conflicts They Inspire," *Newsweek* (August 12, 2002), pp. 44-51.
14. Ibid.
15. Ernest Renan, quoted in Ibn Warraq, *Why I Am Not a Muslim* (Amherst, NY: Prometheus Books, 1995), p. 274.
16. "Islam: Empire of Faith," PBS.
17. Ibid.

18. Ibid.
19. Ibid.
20. Ibid.
21. Ibid.
22. Ibid.
23. Ibid.
24. Caesar E. Farah, *Islam* (Hauppauge, NY: Barron's, 1994), p 452.

CHAPTER EIGHT

OLD TESTAMENT MORALS AND THE KORAN

Mohammed claimed to be a prophet according to the biblical understanding of the term. Thus Jews and Christians had and still have every right to judge his performance as a prophet against biblical standards. Unfortunately, Mohammed's rapacious violence must have made him appear to Jews and Christians in his day as a throwback to the time of the book of Judges and the violent days of King David and his successors.

And Mohammed's tawdry polygamy and sexual exploitation of female slaves must have made him appear to Jews and Christians like an endorser of the wastrel ways of Solomon, the Hebrew king who strayed from the wisdom of his proverb-writing early years into self-indulgent polygamy. Even in the eyes of mature Arab pagans, Mohammed must have looked like a regression from, not a confirmation of, Jewish and Christian standards for a prophet.

None of the major or minor biblical prophets—from Isaiah and Jeremiah to Malachi—are known to have used the sword.

Both Talmudic Judaism and New Testament Christianity—honoring David and Solomon for their Psalms and Proverbs—nonetheless have always expected adherents in subsequent ages to live far above the personal morals of a David or a Solomon. As mentioned earlier, none of the major or minor biblical prophets—from Isaiah and Jeremiah to Malachi—are known to have used the sword, and certainly nowhere in their writings do they urge its use. A very major shift in perspective had occurred (see 1 Chronicles 22:8-9). Instead of men wielding the sword in God's name, devout men leave the sword in God's own hands, to be used in His way and in His time. Mohammed, however, regressed to standards even baser than David's and Solomon's worst deeds. As we have seen, he did so *with a vengeance!*

David, as recorded in Psalm 51, expressed remorse for the sins he committed against Bathsheba, her husband, Uriah, and God. Clearly David did not offer such behavior as an example.

Mohammed, on the other hand, defined even his worst crimes, as weighed against biblical standards, as normative for Muslims.

One higher standard of both Talmudic Judaism and New Testament Christianity is the noble ideal of seeking to influence people, institutions and history by patient charisma and winsome goodwill. In Christianity this progression to a set of standards on a higher plane is expressed remarkably in John 1:17: *"The law was given through Moses; grace and truth came through Jesus Christ."* Though elements within Christendom often slipped back to pre-John 1:17 standards, thank God a flag of remarkable upward progression was planted and, thank God, that flag also is still there.

This Talmudic/New Testament reaching to a higher ideal was either completely over Mohammed's head or was understood but scorned by him. Thus his proteges, imitating his regression to de facto book-of-Judges standards, began spreading Islam by aggression, mayhem, intrigue and military conquest.

And that is precisely the philosophy that radical Muslims, wherever they gain sufficient backing or become a significant majority, feel justified implementing today.

In summary, the Koran, as many quotes in previous chapters reveal, *does* prescribe armed struggle, polygamy and slavery as normative for Muslims *in perpetuity* until Islam becomes **"victorious over every other religion" (Koran 61:9)**. Judaism and Christianity, however, in almost every quarter of the world, have cleansed themselves from past regressions to debased, even savage standards. Yet Muslim and non-Muslim apologists for Islam constantly and ever so illogically exploit Christianity's crusades and inquisitions—scrapped centuries ago—to justify radical Islam's *still current* militancy.

More to the point, was it *really* Christianity that launched crusades and inquisitions, or has the blame for such terrors been misapplied in a centuries-long bad rap?

My next chapter tackles that question.

NEW TESTAMENT MORALS AND THE KORAN

September 11, 2001, suicide bombings in Israel and startling displays of deep-seated hatred of America and the West in Islam-dominated nations have made people stop, think and wonder. What causes such violence in the name of Islam? Is it the belief system itself? The people? The times we live in?

Pundits, commentators and politicians have echoed President George W. Bush's sentiment that the terrorists have hijacked a great, peace-revering religion. Even Senator Hillary Clinton wrote that "we, as a society, too often mischaracterize Islam and those who adhere to its teachings."[1] Given the tidal wave of pro-Islam apologetics that the media are immersing us under and our deeply ingrained Western tendency to want to believe the best, this pattern is not surprising. But be warned: There is an ominously anti-Christian dark side to the secular media's staunchly pro-Muslim onslaught.

A strange idea is gaining acceptance: *You haven't really paid Islam a compliment unless you add a negative comment about Christianity.* PBS's "Islam: Empire of Faith," already reviewed in chapter 7, is a prime example. In ever so many other programs, Muslim spokespersons openly criticize the Bible while media hosts nod and smile. But let a Christian criticize the Koran and media hosts react in a way that would be justified if a swastika had just been painted on a synagogue door.

Much of the Muslim and Western media broadside against Christianity links it with the Inquisition and the Crusades as if these were still in progress. That is an illogical but handy device to lure public attention away from the fact that radical Islam's jihad is *current, active and ongoing.* This is a "now" thing. Again and again we hear the statement, "One can find violence in all religions." Far more pertinent is the closely closeted question: Which religion, if any, is perpetrating violence *now*?

This leads to other equally pertinent questions: *Which religion, if any, tends to be violent because its founding scriptures authorize violence? Which religion, if any, has to violate its own founding scriptures in order to resort to violence?*

I have already demonstrated that Islam's founding charters, the Koran and the hadiths, establish all non-Muslims as the house of war. And the Koran, in more than 100 verses, promotes war, beheadings, slavery and the sexual exploitation of female slaves. Millions of Muslims do not practice what the Koran commands or even what it permits, but it is fair to point out that a call to rapacious violence *is there in the very book they hold in their hands, the book they profess to believe is inspired by God.*

Media attempts to show Christianity as having violence in its founding charter point invariably to the Old Testament. In a recent television interview, Jerry Falwell quoted a war verse from the Koran. Robert Novak, poised and ready, ambushed Rev. Falwell with a quote from the book of Joshua about Israelites slaughtering Canaanites. I tried to "thought-mail" the right answer coast-to-coast into Rev. Falwell's head. I failed. Falwell mumbled an off-the-point answer, leaving Novak barely able to restrain a self-congratulatory smirk.

In the future I hope Christian spokespersons will be clear-headed enough to answer a Novak with "Sir, I am not an Israelite of Joshua's time. I am a Christian who lives by the New Testament. Quote me a New Testament war verse if you can, and I will reply."

IDENTIFYING PSEUDORELIGIONS

Muslims universally regard Islam as *Koran based.* Many Christians similarly plead that Christianity—especially as far as public policy and standards of personal behavior are concerned—be perceived as *New Testament based.* Crusades, an inquisition, rituals, *ex cathedra* pronouncements, traditions and policies accrete around the New Testament, yes, but only as moss grows on a stone. But the moss is not *part of the stone.*

What then of post-New Testament developments that are *called* Christian, but pay only lip service to the New Testament? If such things are not only *not* New Testament-linked, but, far worse, promote anti-New Testament policies, should we still call them Christianity?

The logical answer is, Call all such developments *pseudo-Christianity!*

By the same token, what is called Islam but is not Koran-based is *pseudo-Islam*. Hence violent Christianity is pseudo-Christianity, but oppositely—due to the violent nature of the Koran—*moderate* Islam is *pseudo-Islam*. By "pseudo" I mean not authentic: Something has been altered so antithetically that it no longer resembles the original.

What is called Islam but is not Koran-based is pseudo-Islam.

Distinguishing Christianity from pseudo-Christianity, we recognize the latter—not Christianity—as sourcing inquisitions, crusades, the murder of Jews in sixteenth-century Germany and innocents in twentieth-century Bosnia. To accuse Christianity of advocating crimes of violence, one must first find New Testament verses that teach violence. There are none. Yet Christianity is constantly blamed for pseudo-Christianity's violent crimes.

Kenneth Woodward, in his *Newsweek* article quoted in chapter 7, commendably avoids this unjust blame game. He wrote: "While Crusaders may have fought with the cross on their shields, they did not—could not—cite words from Jesus to justify their slaughters."[2]

Even Ibn Warraq—once a Muslim but now an atheist—admires Jesus' rejection of violence as a weapon that is valid for God's family to use here on Earth. He wrote:

> Western freethinkers, such as [Bertrand] Russell, find Jesus Christ less admirable than Socrates or Buddha. But what do they reproach him with? . . . For cursing a fig tree, causing it to wither and die [Matthew 21:18-21], while

apologists for Islam, Western and Muslim, are trying to excuse *murders* perpetrated by Mohammed [emphasis added].[3]

The Words of Jesus

When Jesus said *"I have come to bring fire on the earth"* (Luke 12:49), He was not proclaiming Himself an arsonist! Bringing spiritual fire to Earth for light, warmth and testing of spiritual qualities is not the same as setting this planet physically aflame. Jesus also said, *"I did not come to bring peace, but a sword"* (Matthew 10:34). By this He meant an ideological sword, one that would divide people having opposite opinions about Him.

Two of Jesus' disciples, brooding because a Samaritan village refused hospitality to Jesus and to them, glowered, *"Lord, do you want us to call down fire from heaven to destroy them?"* (Luke 9:54). How did Jesus respond? He *"turned and rebuked them* [i.e., the two would-be fire-summoners] *and they went to another village"* (Luke 9:55-56).

One may guess—with Koranic passages on violence quoted earlier in mind—how Mohammed would have reacted.

Another time Jesus said to Pontius Pilate, a Roman governor, *"My kingdom is not of this world. If it were, my servants would fight to prevent my arrest"* (John 18:36).

A disciple named Peter once tried to do just that—fight to defend Jesus. Peter struck a presumed enemy with his sword. Jesus immediately healed the wound Peter inflicted. He then rebuked Peter (and any who might follow his example), warning: *"All who draw the sword will also die by the sword"* (Matthew 26:52). The New Testament does agree that civil law enforcement agencies may wield the sword to protect social order in kingdoms of this world (see Romans 13:4). But not one verse in the New Testament authorizes Christians to employ physical weapons in the ministry of the Church. Christian "soldiers" fight on their knees.

Jesus said:

You have heard that it was said, "Love your neighbor and hate your enemy." But I tell you: Love your enemies and pray for those who persecute you, that you may be sons of your Father in heaven (Matthew 5:43-45).

Jesus also said, *"The thief comes only to steal and kill and destroy. I have come that [people] may have life, and have it to the full"* (John 10:10).

The apostle Paul, naming love as the ideal every Christian must seek to emulate, described how that ideal is to be made manifest with these immortal words:

Love is patient, love is kind. . . . It is not easily angered, it keeps no record of wrongs. . . . It always protects, always trusts, always hopes (1 Corinthians 13:4-7).

Consistent with such an exalted concept of love, Paul, echoing Jesus' Sermon on the Mount, wrote:

Bless those who persecute you; bless and do not curse. Do not repay anyone evil for evil. . . . Do not take revenge. . . . If your enemy is hungry, feed him; if he is thirsty, give him something to drink (Romans 12:14-20).

Living and Advancing

When Christians live according to these beautiful New Testament principles Christianity advances throughout the world, overcoming evil by *charisma*, not physical conquest. Islam, applied strictly according to the Koran, relies upon conquest, not charisma.

One major premise found in both Christian and Jewish Scripture clearly explains this ground of *benevolence*, which both religions profess in their very roots, toward every man. The absence

Islam, applied strictly according to the Koran, relies upon conquest, not charisma.

of that premise in the Koran helps explain radical Islam's apparent ground of *malevolence* toward anyone who belongs to Mohammed's house of war rather than to his house of Islam.

In the Likeness of God
That premise is the belief, based on Genesis 1:26-27, that every human being is created in the image (likeness) of God. Even people who deny that they are created in God's likeness are esteemed by devout Jews and Christians as thus created. Hence they too must be treated with dignity and afforded justice. Anyone who is created in the image of God automatically deserves respect but is also viewed as responsible to earn respect.

For James, the Christian apostle who authored a New Testament letter bearing his name, the credo that man is made in the image of God compels Christians also to respect even those whom, by their natural selves, they might prefer to punish, abase or shun. James chidingly wrote, *"With the tongue we praise our Lord and Father, and with it we curse men, who have been made in God's likeness"* (James 3:9).

The Koran contains no evidence that Mohammed believed or had ever even heard of the Bible's man-made-in-the-likeness-of-God doctrine. One can only wonder wistfully what a difference that one highly potent concept might have made in the text of the Koran, if only someone had taught it to Mohammed and if only he had accepted it early enough.

But, due to Mohammed's omission, Muslims tend to believe that describing man as created in the likeness of God is insulting to God.

A Lack of Human Rights

Few Westerners realize how many principles of Western democracies and our justice systems rest upon Genesis 1:26 and James 3:9. The belief that an accused person is innocent until proven guilty is one. The United States Declaration of Independence proclaims that every human being, male and female, are endowed *by their creator* with "certain inalienable rights" and therefore have the right to "life, liberty and the pursuit of happiness."[4]

Correspondingly, Mohammed's failure to embody something resembling James 3:9 in the Koran is a major reason why the Muslim world did not invent democratic freedom for individuals.

Bassam Tibi, a Syrian-born Muslim professor of Islamic Studies at Goettingen University in Germany, in an interview with Indonesia's *Jakarta Post,* said: "The concept of individual human rights is Western. If we [Muslims] say that it is not Western, we are lying to ourselves."[5]

Newsweek ranked 15 Muslim states (there are 55 in the world) according to the degree that they grant individual rights to their citizens. The survey describes the five worst states—Saudi Arabia, Sudan, Libya, Syria and Iraq—as utterly devoid of human rights. It concludes that human rights in seven other states are "few." The three best nations had "some" human rights. Turkey, the most humane, is called "not ideal, but ranks high in the Muslim World." Not even 1 of 55 Muslim nations could be elevated to "ideal."[6]

The Muslim world keeps proving itself unable or unwilling to grant truly democratic freedoms even when dozens of democratic non-Muslim nations are trying to show it how and in some cases even paying it to learn.

SUBMISSION IN ISLAM

Lacking the image-of-God doctrine, Mohammed emphasized something else in its place—submission. The very name he gave to his new religion—*Islam*—means submission. Submission in Islam means submission to God, submission to Mohammed as the ultimate prophet of God, submission to the Koran as the ultimate revelation from God, submission of women to men and submission of everyone to the caliph, sultan, shah or whichever other kind of Muslim ruler is in power.

Hence the same Muslims whom Mohammed taught to fight fiercely against infidels of the house of war are taught to be docile submitters within the house of submission. The problem is that blind, unthinking submission, submission, submission—emphasized over eons of time—does not encourage clearheaded critical thinking, without which no democracy can succeed.

In a submission-focused context, what can voting mean? Dozens of Muslim nations elect parliaments, yes, but to date there is always a strong man who can demand submission from the entire body of elected officials at will. Those who refuse to submit risk assassination.

The Value of a Muslim

A devout Muslim's sense of his own intrinsic value, accordingly, does not rest upon recognition of God's likeness within him. He measures it instead by the intensity of his uncritical submission to every requirement of the Koran. The opening verse of the Koran's first major chapter, chapter 2, proclaims the Koran as a book that is **"not to be doubted."**

Were it not so, books as critical as this one would have been written by Muslims themselves centuries ago. It should not have been left to an outsider such as me. Or does it take an outsider to see certain things more clearly?

The Question of Polygamy

How appealingly the New Testament differs from Mohammed's onerous endorsement of violence, polygamy, slavery and the sexual exploitation of slaves. Paul the apostle, writing to his protege Timothy in a day when polygamy was common, ruled that overseers of Christian congregations must be *"above reproach, the husband of but one wife, temperate, self-controlled . . . not violent but gentle, not quarrelsome, not a lover of money* [or plunder!]" (1 Timothy 3:2-3).

Obviously Mohammed would not have qualified.

Paul's 2,000-year-old rule that overseers of Christian congregations must set an example for monogamy initiated a social trend that led eventually to monogamy being upheld as the only legal form of marriage in all of today's Western democracies.

Christianity has always remained content with Paul's monogamy-for-overseers rule, which—by the power of a good example—gradually became a monogamy-for-all-Christians rule.

The Issue of Slavery

Critics of Christianity often claim that the New Testament—like the Koran—does not condemn slavery. But it does. In 1 Timothy 1:8-10, Paul listed lawbreakers whom God's Old Testament law is meant to restrain. Paul's list includes, among other wrongdoers, adulterers and slave traders.

Paul sought to counteract slavery by attacking its source— slave trading. If slave trading is abolished, slave taking, sans the incentive of financial gain, will also end. Meanwhile—until that long-term goal is accomplished—since adultery is proscribed, sex with existing slaves is also forbidden.

Paul then declared slave trading and everything else on that ignominious list as contrary not only to Old Testament law, but also to *"the glorious gospel of the blessed God"* (1 Timothy 1:11).

TAMPERING WITH SCRIPTURE

Fifteen times in the Koran Mohammed confidently claimed that God gave him the Koran to *confirm* Jewish law and the Christian gospel. He attributed this quote to God: **"We have sent down the Koran to you with truth confirmatory of previous scriptures,** [i.e., the Old and New Testaments] **and as their safeguard"** **(Koran 5:52).**

With a **"safeguard"** like the Koran, surely the Bible needs no attacker! Islam's hadiths mention a man who as a youth fought alongside Mohammed. Asked how often he actually accompanied the so-called prophet to battle or on raids, the veteran replied, "Nineteen times."[7]

We can hardly expect a body of scripture coming from so violent a prophet to inspire peace and harmony.

Other sources claim Mohammed personally led 27 out of 65 military campaigns that he plotted against Jews, Christians and other Arabs who refused to acknowledge him as a prophet.

We can hardly expect a body of scripture coming from so violent a prophet to inspire peace and harmony between Muslims and non-Muslims. Indeed, a spirit of bellicosity toward non-Muslims rankles in nearly half of the Koran's longer chapters.

A Muslim once voiced a complaint to me. "Christians and Jews," he said, "freely acknowledge their common origin when they speak of Judeo-Christianity. Islam comes from the same root. Why can't Islam be included? Why not say *Judeo-Christo-Islam?*"

Apart from writing this book, how could I explain to him the many reasons why I could not agree? One easy-to-explain reason is, Christianity accepts the Old Testament *as it is*! Islam does not. Christians do not revise the Old Testament, tout their revisions as the original and then blame the Jews for failing to make their Scriptures match revisions Christians would make centuries later.

Deleting something as major as the Passover from his 27 tellings of the Exodus story, as I have already noted, is just one of hundreds of ways Mohammed desecrated the Old Testament while claiming to confirm it.

Islam, moreover, would never allow its name to occupy the third slot, following Judeo-Christo. Muslims claim that Islam began with Abraham and Ishmael, and thus is older than both Judaism and Christianity. Little did my Muslim acquaintance dream how utterly opposed everyone—Jews, Christians *and Muslims*—would be to his suggestion.

The Koran and the Virgin Birth

Mohammed's tampering with the New Testament rates no better. Sternly rejecting the deity of Jesus Christ, Mohammed still deigned to confess His virgin birth (see Koran 3:45-47; 19:16-21, *Arberry*). Most Muslims fudge their translation of all three passages, yet the Koran always and only calls Jesus **"the son of Mary" (Koran 2:87** and others) and *never* mentions Joseph nor any other male as Jesus' father. Instead, even M. M. Ali—ever eager to extol Mohammed and downgrade Jesus—has an angel assure a confused Mary: **"Allah creates what he pleases. When he decrees a matter, he only says to it, Be, and it is" (Koran 3:46).**

Miraculous conception! The same miracle is found again in Arberry's translation: **"[Mary] guarded her virginity, so We breathed into her of Our spirit, and appointed her and her son as a sign to all beings" (Koran 21:91).**

The miraculous conception again—given as a **"sign"** to all mankind. Yet Islam forever labors to obscure that sign's awesome significance.

Only one verse notes a man other than elderly Zachariah (see Koran 3:37) attending to Mary at all near the time she conceived: **"We sent unto her Our Spirit that presented himself to her a man without fault" (Koran 19:17, *Arberry*).** Again, the man was not an actual *man* but God's Spirit.

> ### Since God caused Jesus to be conceived miraculously, surely we may refer to God as Jesus' Father.

As surely as there is a conception, there must be two parents. Since God caused Jesus to be conceived miraculously, surely we may refer to God as Jesus' Father and Jesus as God's Son, acknowledging of course that physical intercourse was not involved. That is part of what Christianity has always taught, yet Muslims, moderates included, commonly accuse Christians of teaching that God had intercourse with Mary.

When a father begets a son physically, he transmits his DNA, his likeness, his strength, to his son. As surely as God fathered Jesus *spiritually,* by the Koran's own admission (see Koran 21:91), features of deity—sinlessness, ability to create life, ability to work humanly impossible miracles and so on—would have been transmitted to Jesus. Does the Koran attest the transmission of such capacities from God to Jesus? Indeed it does.

Jesus in the Koran

The Koran implies that Jesus was sinless. In verse 19:19, in Arberry's translation, God's Spirit informs Mary that her son will be **"a boy most pure."** By contrast, the Koran describes various other prophets acknowledging their sins or praying for forgiveness—*including Mohammed!*

Muslim translator Ahmed Ali has God commanding Mohammed to **"seek forgiveness for your sins" (Koran 40:55)**. Dawood's translation of the same verse concurs with **"implore forgiveness for your sins."** Arberry and Marmaduke Pickethall both have **"Ask forgiveness for your sin."** Rodwell has **"seek pardon for thy fault."** M. M. Ali, ever on duty to defend Mohammed, even if implausibly, changes the sense to **"ask protection for thy sin."** Why would God want to protect someone's sin? M. Z. Khan strays entirely with **"ask forgiveness for those who wrong thee."**

(Perhaps Mr. Khan hasn't noticed that Mohammed preferred just to *kill* those who wronged him.)

Yet not even one phrase of one verse in the Koran links Jesus with sin of any kind.

Among all the prophets the Koran mentions, it uniquely ascribes to Jesus the ability to give life to inanimate matter. He made a clay bird, and when He breathed on it, it became a living bird (see Koran 5:110). The same verse attests that Jesus gave sight to the blind, healed lepers and even raised the dead back to life! Characteristics of the heavenly Father were indeed showing up in the Son.

Mohammed also ascribed two amazing titles to Jesus**: "the Word from God" (Koran 3:39)** and a **"Spirit from him" (Koran 4:171)**. These two unique titles imply that Jesus is much more than a man. To be the Word from and a Spirit coming from God, Jesus had to exist with God *before* He became human, contrary to Islamic dogma.

And yet, after acknowledging this much about Jesus, Mohammed chose to deny Jesus' atoning death and resurrection, eviscerating the very heart right out of the New Testament gospel.

These are just a few of ever so many reasons why any expression such as *Judeo-Christo-Islam* can only be rejected as a travesty.

Notes

1. Hillary Clinton, "Islam in America," *Chicago Sun-Times*, February 25, 1996, n.p.
2. Kenneth L. Woodward, "The Bible and the Qur'an," *Newsweek* (February 11, 2002), p. 53.
3. Ibn Warraq, *Why I Am Not a Muslim* (Amherst, NY: Prometheus Books, 1995), p. 350.
4. The Thirteen United States of America, Declaration of Independence, 1776.
5. Mochtar Buchori, "Secularization: An Extention of the Idea of the Primacy of Reason," *Jakarta Post* (December 22, 1998), p. 5.
6. "Freedom Barely Rings," *Newsweek* (December 22, 2001), p. 25.
7. The hadiths (n.p.).

A WARRING PROPHET'S SUPREMACIST LEGACY

Just as Mohammed personified militancy at Islam's beginning, his example and his Koran subsequently inspired more of the same. In the decades following Mohammed's A.D. 632 death, Muslim armies overran Jerusalem, Alexandria, Antioch and Carthage.

Eventually Islamic forces controlled all of North Africa, Syria, Asia Minor, Spain and Portugal. A Muslim army invaded France, reaching to within 300 miles of the south coast of England.

There, at last, Charles Martel and his army of Franks stopped them in the Battle of Tours in 732–100 years after Mohammed's death. Subsequent battles enabled Europeans to reclaim Spain and Portugal, but Asia Minor, all of North Africa and large parts of the Middle East remained captive.

Centuries later a second major Muslim attempt to gain control of all of Europe brought a Turkish army up through the Balkans to besiege Vienna, Austria. The year was 1683. The Turks were finally defeated and turned back on *September 11!* Still the Turks kept parts of the Balkans under Muslim domination.

The first Islamic invasion of Europe, which I call the initial century-long Islamic holocaust, cannot be construed as simply a Muslim reaction to the Crusades. The Crusades, ill-advised and horrible as they were, came much later. They were a long-delayed European attempt to secure only the Holy Land as a safe destination for Christian pilgrims.

Islam's initial advance out of Arabia was virtually unopposed, yet Muslim armies slaughtered thousands of Jews, Christians and pagans who, while not resisting militarily, simply resisted conversion to Islam. Historian Bat Ye'or describes the horrors that occurred:

> The Arab conquest was accompanied by tremendous destruction. Christian sources, but Muslim chronicles even more so, describe entire towns, innumerable villages given over to pillage and fire, to massacres, slavery and deportation of populations. Even towns provided with a treaty of protection in exchange for surrendering without resistance did not escape pillage by Arab tribes fascinated by the immensity of the booty.[1]

All this in the name of a religion claiming to be an improvement over everything that ever preceded it.

Once the Muslim killers and plunderers were sated and began to weary of atrocity, a more orderly—but no less despotic—method of jihad was formulated. Ye'or describes how thoroughly the Koran itself dictated that formulation:

The general basic principles according to the Koran are as follows: the pre-eminence of Islam over all other religions (9:33); Islam is the true religion of Allah (3:17) and it should reign over all mankind (34:27); the *umma* [Muslim community] forms the party of Allah

Dead people cannot pay revenue, so murder gave way to oppressive taxation.

and is perfect (3:106), having been chosen above all peoples on earth it alone is qualified to rule, and thus elected by Allah to guide the world (35:37). The pursuit of jihad, until this goal will be achieved, is an obligation (8:40). The religions of the Bible and Zoroastrianism are deemed inferior as their followers falsified the true Revelation which their respective prophets conveyed to them—this revelation was considered to be Islam—before Mohammed's arrival. . . . These peoples, each a beneficiary of [earlier] revelation, have the choice between war or submission to the *umma*, whereas idolaters are forced to convert to Islam or be killed. . . . Either the individual or the tribe would convert to Islam . . . or conversion was replaced by the payment of a tribute.[2]

By "tribute," the translator of Bat Ye'or's French means not a one-time payment but a *jizya*, i.e., a tax that is collectible in perpetuity.

In other words, Muslims remembered an option Mohammed adopted while conquering a tribe of Jews at a settlement called Kaybar. It was the option of killing (only *some*) enough infidels to gain control, but sparing others to be heavily taxed (see Koran 9:29). Dead people cannot pay revenue, so murder gave way to oppressive taxation. Fewer and fewer Jews and Christians were forced to convert to Islam, because those left unconverted could be subjected to unconscionable extortion, as Bat Ye'or describes:

> The *jizya* was a poll tax assessed at three rates: 12, 24 or 48 *dirhams*, depending on the taxpayer's economic situation. . . . For the Shafi'ites: "Our religion compels the poll tax to be paid by dying people, the old, even in a state of incapacity, the blind, monks, workers and the poor, incapable of practicing a trade."
>
> Anyone [i.e., any non-Muslim] who left their homes without their receipt for the *jizya*, or who had lost it, incurred the greatest danger. In the Ottoman empire the receipt had to be produced on pain of immediate imprisonment, at the demand of tax collectors who stopped *dhimmis* [non-Muslims]—recognizable by their distinctive dress—in the street.[3]

The jizya was not the only basic tax exacted from dhimmis. Bat Ye'or continues:

> All taxes paid on trade and transport by Muslims were generally doubled for *dhimmis*. In addition, the population— but particularly the *dhimmi* communities—were subject to ruinous extortions designed to cover the financing of

incessant wars. . . . Fiscal oppression . . . was a primary cause of the disappearance of large numbers of *dhimmi* populations through conversion to Islam or flight.[4]

One cannot but ask why did not *all* Jews, Christians and Zoroastrians who for eons were enduring Islam's intolerable discrimination simply convert to Islam and be done with it? Why flee when flight limited a fugitive to take only what he could carry? Why flee when flight might mean nothing more than leaping from the frying pan of Muslim oppression in one region into the fire of even worse Muslim oppression in another? There can be only one answer to that why. Those dhimmis who steadfastly refused to convert did so because they loathed Mohammed, loathed the Koran and loathed Islam even more than they feared and resented the oppression of all three.

A certain kind of ant is said to keep aphids captive deep inside its nests in order to milk them. Muslims, like these ants, adopted a strategy of milking Jews and Christians as "cash aphids." But there is a major difference: Aphids are perhaps content under ant control whereas dhimmis under Muslim oppression *suffered*!

Yet to some outsiders in the West, it appeared that Islam was actually tolerant of Jews and Christians. Muslim apologists have been quick to feed that misperception, hoping to keep it alive. For many decades Western historical researchers—accepting Muslim apologists' reports at face value—credited Islam with tolerance toward Jews and Christians. Only in recent decades has independent research, led especially by Bat Ye'or and Bernard Lewis, uncovered the manifold cruelty and continuous economic oppression that Muslims inflicted upon Jews and Christians in Muslim-controlled areas from the 700s onward.

Drawing extensively from still another treatise by Bat Ye'or *The Dhimmi: Jews and Christians Under Islam* and six different books on the topic by Bernard Lewis, former Muslim Ibn Warraq describes how centuries of Islamic oppression functioned. The following quotes from Warraq's *Why I Am Not a Muslim* are truly stereotype-shattering:

> Muhammad's treatment of the Jews at the Oasis of Kaybar served "as a model for the treaties granted by Arab conquerors to conquered peoples in territories beyond Arabia." Muhammad attacked the oasis in 628, had one of the leaders [of the Jews] tortured to find the hidden treasures of the tribe. When the Jews surrendered, he agreed to let them continue cultivating their oasis only if they gave him half their produce. Muhammad also reserved the right to cancel the treaty and expel the Jews whenever he liked. This treaty was called a "dhimma," and those who accepted it were known as "dhimmis." All non-Muslims who accepted Muslim supremacy and agreed to pay tribute [were thereafter known as] "dhimmis."[5]

Paying tribute was not the only ignominy:

> In all litigation between a Muslim and a dhimmi, the validity of the oath or testimony of a dhimmi was not recognized. . . . Since a dhimmi could not give evidence against a Muslim, the Muslim opponent always got off scot-free. The dhimmi was forced to bribe his way out of [a trial]. . . . Any fine imposed upon a Muslim was halved if the victim was a dhimmi. . . . Accusations of blasphemy against dhimmis were frequent and the penalty was capital punishment. . . . In practice if not in law, a dhimmi would often be sentenced to death if he dared raise his hand against a Muslim, even in self-defense." Even an

accidental killing of a Muslim could condemn [an entire dhimmi] community to death or exile.[6]

A Muslim caliph, Umar ben Abd al-Aziz, who ruled from A.D. 717 to A.D. 720, created a list of rules which he and his successors compelled dhimmis to obey. The list, known as the Pact of Umar, forced dhimmis to promise to honor regulations such as the following:

> We will not build . . . any new monasteries, churches, hermitages or monks' cells. We will not restore . . . any that have fallen into ruin or are located in a Muslim quarter.
> We will provide three days food and lodging to any Muslims who pass our way.
> We will not hold public religious ceremonies. We will not proselytise. We will not prevent any of our kin from embracing Islam if they so desire. . . . We shall offer our seats when [Muslims] wish to be seated.
> We will not ride on saddles. We will not wear swords or carry weapons of any kind. . . . We will not build our homes higher than [the homes of Muslims].[7]

The dhimmis were in constant danger of being enslaved. Ibn Warraq explains:

> When Amr conquered Tripoli in 643, he forced Jews and Christians to hand over their women and children as slaves to the Arab army. . . . They were told to deduct this "handover" from the poll tax, the dread "jizya."[8]

We are not told how large or how small a tax deduction a man was permitted to take for the loss of his wife or a child. Warraq continues:

Between 652 and 1276, Nubia [now called Sudan] was forced to send an annual contingent of slaves to Cairo. The treaties concluded under the Umayyads and the Abbasids [two different dynasties of Muslim rulers] with the towns of Trans-oxiana, Sijistan, Armenia and Fezzan (modern northwest Africa) all stipulated an annual tribute of slaves of both sexes. . . . In 781, at the sack of Ephesus, 7,000 Greeks were deported into captivity. After the capture of Amorium in 838, there were so many captives that the Caliph al-Mutasim ordered them auctioned in batches of 5 and 10. At the sack of Thessalonica in 903, 22,000 Christians were divided among the Arab chieftans or sold into slavery. In 1064, the Seljuk Sultan, Alp Arslan, devasted Georgia and Armenia. Those he did not take as prisoners he executed.[9]

Another crushing oppression Islam imposed upon Christians beginning in the mid-1300s under an Ottoman Sultan named Orkhan was called *devshirme*. It consisted of

A periodic taking of one-fifth of all Christian children in the conquered territories. Converted to Islam, these children [when they reached the age] of 14, were trained to be janissaries or infantry men. These periodic abductions eventually became annual. . . . The system was open to all kinds of abuse. [Collection] agents often took more than the required number and sold the "surplus" children back to their parents. . . . This [system] was abolished in 1656, [but was replaced by an alternate arrangement] in which young children, between the ages of 6 to 10, were taken to be trained in the seraglio [harem] of the sultan . . . [this] continued until the 18th century.[10]

Next, Warraq addresses the matter of massive forced conversions into the ranks of Islam:

> Islamic history is full of references to the forced conversion of Christians, [Jews, mentioned earlier] Zoroastrians and pagans.[11]

Warraq gives examples too numerous to quote and almost too horrifying to be read without weeping.

Yes, the crusaders inflicted their atrocities too—during a briefer span of history and partially in retaliation for Islamic atrocities such as some of the above—atrocities widely recited in those days, only to be forgotten by most Christians centuries later. The major difference is this: Crusader atrocities *contradicted* the New Testament whereas Muslim atrocities were *in accord with* the Koran.

Crusader atrocities *contradicted* the New Testament whereas Muslim atrocities were *in accord with* the Koran.

I leave it to readers to peruse further the works of Bat Ye'or, Bernard Lewis and Ibn Warraq for stockpiles of still more historical evidence that shatters the myth of Islamic rule as *admirably tolerant* of Jewish, Christian, Zoroastrian and pagan minorities. Other oppressors, oppressing for a generation or two, faded from history's pages, leaving the oppressed to recover. Islamic supremacism sustained its horrible oppressions over more than a millennium.

For example, Muslim apologists make much of the fact that some Jews, facing calamities such as pseudo-Christianity's horrid Inquisition in Europe, fled to Muslim North Africa for relief. They preferred to pay Islam's extortionary high taxes rather than be killed. True, but pseudo-Christianity's times of madness happened only for a decade or two at a time—separated often by a century or two of peaceful coexistence with Jews. Islam's oppression of Jews by extortionary taxation, by contrast, was constant. Its stealing of Jewish children from their families was almost as constant and continued over centuries.

Thus, as Bat Ye'or verifies, European Jews *rarely* fled south to Muslim North Africa. It was far more common for North African Jews to flee *north* to Christian Europe.

I turn next to focus on how *modern* Muslims are seeking to restore Islamic supremacism in today's world.

Notes

1. Bat Ye'or, *Islam and Dhimmitude: Where Civilizations Collide* (Cranbury, NJ: Associated University Presses, 2002), p. 48.
2. Ibid., p. 41.
3. Ibid., p. 69.
4. Ibid., p. 71.
5. Ibn Warraq, *Why I Am Not a Muslim* (Amherst, NY: Prometheus Books, 1995), p. 217.
6 Ibid., p. 229.
7. Ibid., p. 230.
8. Ibid., p. 231.
9. Ibid.
10. Ibid.
11. Ibid., p. 231.

CHAPTER ELEVEN

ISLAM'S PLAN FOR WORLD DOMINATION

Mohammed could not have known the size of the world, but several passages in the Koran show that he envisioned Islam dominating all of it, however large it might be: **"He it is who sent his messenger . . . that he may cause it** [Islam] **to prevail over all religions" (Koran 9:33, *M. M.Ali*;** see also 48:28 and 61:9**).** M. M. Ali designates these three passages as "the prophecy of the ultimate triumph of Islam in the whole world."[1]

Mohammed's successors, the caliphs, quoted passages like these to inspire Muslim armies as they advanced out of Arabia, imposing Islam by the sword upon a peacefully unsuspecting Middle East and North Africa, as I describe in the previous chapter.

Islamic armies, imbued with what Mohammed claimed was divine authorization, imposed Islam by force over vast areas, all the while extorting wealth from subjugated Jews and Christians to fund their ongoing conquests. As I noted, major defeats at Tours, France, in A.D. 732, and again at Vienna, Austria, in A.D. 1683, halted Islam's attempt to take all of Europe by force. Gradually Islamic forces were forced to retreat from Europe, except for part of the Balkans. But Islam has again set its sights on a conquest of Europe and of European civilization, wherever the latter has spread to North and South America and other regions. Muslim strategists ask their followers, *Why do we find in these modern times that Allah has entrusted most of the world's oil wealth primarily to Muslim nations?*

Their answer: Allah foresaw Islam's need for funds to finance a final politico-religious victory over what Islam perceives as its ultimate enemy: Christianized Euro-American civilization. So, Islam follows Nazism, fascism and communism as the world's latest hostile takeover aspirant.

Nazis, fascists and communists failed. Does Islam have a better chance at success? I believe it will flounder if we awaken to its threat in time; yet, if there is not adequate planned resistance, Islam does have a better chance of succeeding. Communism's world takeover attempt was guaranteed to fail because its economic policy was naively contrary to human nature. Advocating the rubric *What is mine is thine, and what is thine is mine*, communism failed to see that human nature *will not* keep those two balanced propositions in equilibrium. Like a female black widow spider consuming her mate, the latter part of the formula makes a meal of the former, leading to the collapse of any system based upon that formula.

In contrast, political systems do well if they can persuade people to adhere to *What's mine is mine* and *What's thine is thine* maxims.

Only if a strong religious incentive is added does such an idealistic formula have any long-term chance. Even then success will be spotty. But communism (and Nazism, for that matter) excluded religion. And *that* mistake was the final nail eventually clamping a lid on communism's coffin. Communism, on a historical scale, perished while still in its childhood.

Islam is not repeating communism's mistake. Mating political cunning and incredible wealth with religious zeal, Islam *does* have a chance to succeed and *will* succeed unless major parts of the Western world unite to take appropriate countermeasures. But many Western leaders, unable to believe that a mere religion could possibly be a serious political threat, keep proclaiming themselves as Islam-friendly, reasoning that all religions are good—*aren't they?*

A Muslim strategist in Beverly Hills, California, declared several years ago, as quoted by a friend of mine: "Now that the struggle between Western democracies and international communism is winding down, it is time for the real and final struggle to begin, and *we are going to win!*"[2]

When will people realize that just as there are good doctors and quacks, good cops and rogue cops, there can also be good religions and bad religions?

KEY ISLAMIC STRATEGIES

Here are some of Islam's primary strategies:

Exploit Massive Immigration—Legal and Illegal—of Muslims into Western Nations

A faction of Islamic leaders in Great Britain waited until about 1 million Muslims had immigrated to or otherwise managed to infiltrate the country. Then they boldly announced the establishment of an Islamic parliament. Britons urged Muslims to call it an *association,* a *foundation,* a *society*—anything but a parliament.[3] But Muslim leaders remain adamant. Their parliament is already passing laws that Muslims in Great Britain are required to obey. No one doubts that key Muslims in the British Isles intend their upstart parliament, at some point, to replace Great Britain's time-honored institution. Ibn Warraq comments:

> Undoubtedly the most articulate advocate of a theocratic Islamic world order is Dr. Kalim Siddiqui. . . . He was one of the founding members of the so-called Muslim Parliament of Great Britain, whose aim is to "define, defend and promote the Muslim interest in Britain." [He] has written an enormous number of books and articles on Islam and its mission in the west and in the world. Constantly recurring themes are the coming Islamic global dominion, the greatness of the Ayatollah Khomeini, the need for an armed struggle . . . and the indivisible unity of religion and politics. . . . [Siddiqui says,] "With a population of almost one billion [*more* than 1 billion now] and infinite sources of wealth, you can defeat all the powers."[4]

Ibn Warraq also explains that Dr. Kalim Siddiqui, director of the Muslim Institute in London, around the time that Muslims across Europe were venting utter rage over Salman Rushdie's *The Satanic Verses* with "riots, demonstrations and book burnings," urged a Muslim crowd at a public meeting "not to obey British laws if they went against the Sharia, the Islamic law."[5] Under Sharia law, Rushdie, of course, had to be assassinated. Warraq adds:

> Many Muslims have made it clear that they have no intention of being assimilated into the [British] host society;

instead, it is up to the host society to change, to accord them separate rights, separate privileges. Some of their most articulate spokesmen have spelled out what they hope to achieve. Dr. Zaki Badawi, former director of the Islamic Cultural Center, London, wrote: "Islam intends to expand in Britain. Islam is a universal religion. It aims at bringing its message to all corners of the earth. It hopes that one day the whole of humanity will be one Muslim community, the *Umma*."[6]

This utter brashness of Muslims in Great Britain has been encouraged by inexcusable timidity on the part of the British police and general malaise among Britons. Ibn Warraq protests: "Scandalously, the British police did not take a single step to arrest Muslims who were publicly advocating the murder of Rushdie [a British citizen]."[7]

In France, contrastingly, "a Turkish imam [a priest of Islam] who claimed that the Sharia had precedence over French laws was deported within forty-eight hours!"[8]

A Behind-the-Scenes Takeover
Let us not think, however, that an absence of public brashness by Muslims equates with docility. Muslims in other nations can be just as fanatically wedded to the goals of a Siddiqui and a Badawi, but seek subtle, behind-the-scenes ways of reaching the same objectives. The following scenario explains how I *think* Islam is most likely to progress, if it is allowed, toward its ultimate goal: a takeover of the world.

It is only a matter of time. As Muslim immigrants continue flooding into Western nations, some of them will candidate for and eventually win more and more seats in the parliaments of Western nations that have chosen parliamentary-style democratic government. Eventually, a duly-elected Muslim will be ensconced as prime minister of a parliamentary Western democracy. Should that Muslim prime minister happen to be a closet Islamic supremacist, democracy in the nation concerned will have very obligingly stretched out its neck under a guillotine.

Recognizing that a critical mass among Canada's fine citizenry holds ultraliberal views, I fear that Canada will perhaps be the first Western nation to spring a supremacist Islamic trap on its own foot. (I write as one who holds Canadian as well as U.S. citizenship.)

There is a reason why a Muslim is more likely to become a prime minister of a parliamentary Western government before a Muslim becomes a *president* of a Western republic such as the United States of America. Under parliamentary government, voters vote for the political party that they favor, more than for the leader of that party. The choice of an actual leader is primarily the winning party's privilege. In a republic, the selection of *the* leader is a separate election issue. A presidential candidate may be rejected by voters even though they favor the party he leads. This difference subjects a presidential candidate in a republic to much more intense public scrutiny than a candidate for a prime minister's office normally faces.

Once a supremacist Muslim becomes a prime minister of a Western nation, wealthy oil-producing Muslim interests become a de facto ghost cabinet at his side. External oil money, supplementing internal revenue, virtually guarantees the success of his social programs. In time he will offer to arbitrate political turmoil in the Middle East and lo! his efforts will succeed amazingly (though only for a strategic interval) where a George Bush or a Colin Powell failed. This ploy will suggest to the Western world that the way to ease tensions between the West and the Islamic world is to have more Muslims as heads of Western governments, because other *Muslims listen to them.*

Of course they do! Each success the new Muslim prime minister enjoys at home or abroad adds to his reputation and gains favor for the religion he represents. Bribes enabled by foreign oil money may not be out of the question.

Under his government, public-school curricula sprout lessons extolling Islam and debasing other religions. Under his leadership, immigration policies favor still more waves of Muslim immigrants, guaranteeing ever larger Islamic bloc votes for him and for other Muslim candidates for political office. Eventually, perhaps in his second term, he appoints Muslims as heads of departments, even as *heads of the armed forces.*

The parliament he leads begins to change existing laws and create new ones, all with a view to moving the nation he heads ever closer to an eventual full imposition of Islam's ultraharsh Sharia code of law. Designating female genital mutilation (FGM) as an operation that Western doctors may legally perform on Muslim women will probably be first. Some doctors will welcome the extra income for such an *easy* surgery, just as some of them bank extra income for performing unnecessary abortions now.

Apart from a strong public outcry against FGM, the next change proposed will be to legalize what will perhaps by then be called *quadrogamy* (or will it be *quadrogeny?*). Islam permits one man to wed as many as *four* women, hence—*quadrogamy!* But as surely as the new ruling applies only for *Muslim* males, several million Western males who are little more than brutish pagans anyway—cheering the new law in—will line up and convert to Islam simply to enjoy more sex under the ruling.

Thus Mohammed's seventh-century calumny—indulging the male sex drive as a ploy to entice pagan males into his fold—will serve radical Islam again in a twenty-first-century context. Simultaneously, magazine articles galore will gush specious assurance to Western women that quadrogamy may actually be good for them as well.

At some point, Islam's Friday officially replaces Christianity's Sunday as the primary day of religious observance during the week, although Islam itself has no day of rest. Another act, allowing Islam to enforce its own religious punishment for apostates, follows—another progression toward shoe-horning Islam's ultra-harsh *Sharia law* into an already parasitized Western nation.

Perhaps last of all, what is now castigated universally as *white slavery* (not that it is in any worse or better than *black* slavery) will be subtly redefined as a testable solution to poverty.

The argument will run: Which is better for undereducated, underprivileged people? To serve someone else without pay but be clothed, fed and sheltered—or for him or her to wander hopelessly as a street person? Thus Mohammed's seventh-century endorsement of slavery will resurrect to haunt the modern world as the initial narrow justification for reintroducing slavery widens later.

At some point in this scenario, oil-rich Muslim nations begin making enticing offers to banks, especially to banks in the first Muslim-led Western nation. Oil-rich potentates offer to deposit 1 million dollars in low-interest term deposits for every 5 or 10 Muslim employees a given bank can show it has hired nationwide. They promise to add still more million-dollar deposits for every Muslim employee that the bank can show it has promoted to a managerial position. They add further million-dollar deposits for every qualified Muslim the bank can show it has promoted to a high-level managerial position.

Would any bank refuse, since such an arrangement would all be quite legal? As a result, banks in the nation scenarioed prosper. Interest rates drop and the economy booms. And the supremacist Muslim prime minister claims credit for it all, while his ghost cabinet grins. And the world looks on, impressed.

Would a congressional inquiry find this last ploy already happening in the United States? If it is or isn't, it must be declared illegal *now!* Every government guards against foreign interference in its *politics*. What about guarding against meddlesome foreign interference with customarily open domestic hiring policies? Banks eager for deposits, industries eager for sales, hospitals or colleges eager for donations—all could become incalculably biased in favor of Islam.

Like everyone else, enterprising Muslims seek to better themselves in our economies. But let them do so on a level playing field. Watchdog groups justifiably blow the whistle against *racial* bias in hiring. What about a hiring policy that is secretly biased according to *religion*?

If, in the economy at large, Muslims begin popping up with unusual frequency as CEOs of banks, the media, hospitals and myriad other institutions, and if most Muslim CEOs, once situated, begin giving preference to Muslims for employment, conversion to Islam will quickly be recognized as a major career enhancer. Finally, when it is too late, supremacist Islam's crassest denials of human rights will begin to emerge under darkening skies.

Part of this conjectural scenario is already detectable in the United States. One example: A Christian nurse in Pennsylvania told me that the head doctor in a hospital where she worked retired and was replaced by a Muslim doctor. The Muslim quickly fired her and two other nurses who were known to be Christians. He replaced them with Muslim nurses. Then he began gradually dismissing other nurses and replacing them with Muslims as well.

Parts of this scenario (and worse) are also already happening internationally, especially for Christian minorities in Muslim nations. In Indonesia, Batak Christians employed in government or in other institutions in Medan—the largest city on the Indonesian island called Sumatra—are fired from their jobs and then told, "If you want to be rehired, come back as a Muslim."

Muslim mobs burn Indonesian churches. When Christians collect offerings to rebuild, Muslims in the local building-permit office announce that the zoning laws have changed, hence a church cannot be built there now. So Christians rent commercial space in which to worship, only to have Muslim police burst in, demanding to see a permit to use commercial space for a religious purpose (a permit which Muslim authorities may withhold even if it is requested). Without a permit, Christians see pews, Bibles and hymnbooks dragged out into the street and burned. On Christmas Eve 2000, Muslim homemade bombs killed dozens of worshipers in Indonesian church services.[9]

How would the above scenario conclude? It would likely end with parts of the population of the United States of America—the last bastion—feeling the pull of the Islamic siren that by then has already seduced many of America's allies across the Western world. A supremacist Muslim candidate would run for president. Foreign oil money would saturate the media with his political ads. If he won, the world would be changed forever, apart from divine intervention by a deity far more worthy to be worshiped than the Koran's Allah.

Every reader of the above scenario—Protestant, Catholic, Jew, Hindu, Buddhist or humanist—must ask his or her own being—*am I willing to let the world I live in be transmogrified by Islam?* Even those who doubt that anything like the above scenario can happen should ask, *What should I do now just in case?*

A major supremacist Muslim strategy, then, is first to get large numbers of Muslims in as immigrants—including Muslim immigrants who are unaware of the infiltration scheme—and then to help them gain advantages in every possible way over the original society of the nation to be parasitized.

Widening Islamic Influence
There are other subtleties. Again, we go to England.

A Muslim organization wanted to build an enormous Islamic studies center virtually next door to prestigious Oxford University. The Muslim planners requested Oxford to sell them a choice block of land that Oxford was reserving for its own future expansion.

Oxford refused to sell.

Undeterred, the Muslims called upon a prestigious Muslim gentlemen's club to invite Prince Charles into its membership. He accepted the "honor," only to find that as the club's newest member, he was expected to show loyalty and magnanimity by using his clout as the Prince of Wales to persuade Oxford to sell

Naive Europeans who *think* they are showing tolerance to a mere religion are actually inviting a very potent *political* invader into their societies.

the land to the Muslim planners. Prince Charles complied. He pressured Oxford. Oxford sold the land. The new Islamic studies center is perhaps by now already completed.

In a thousand different ways naive Europeans who *think* they are showing noble tolerance to a mere religion are actually inviting a very potent *political* invader into their societies. Blasé immigration officials are steadily undoing the victory Charles Martel and the Franks so bravely won for us at Tours, and which the Habsburgs won for us again at Vienna.

Naiveté can be the most devastating betrayer of all.

A Multibillion Dollar International Mosque-Construction and Koran-Translation Program

The burgeoning success that Christian missions achieved by surrounding the Muslim world with hundreds of millions of third-world Christians worshiping in hundreds of thousands of third-world churches has caught the eye of Muslim strategists. Launching a massive attempt to "catch up" missionary-wise, oil-rich Muslim nations are now spending billions constructing mosques in hundreds of cities of the non-Muslim world—cities they showed no interest in until these last few decades.

Mosque building in hundreds of cities of sub-Saharan and southern Africa has been underway for years. Now it is also happening almost everywhere in Latin America and Australia.

The largest of dozens of magnificent mosques newly built up and down South America stands in downtown Caracas, Venezuela. I have seen mosques even in smaller cities of Brazil (Juan Pesoes, Natal, Recife), not to mention major cities such as Rio de Janeiro, Sao Paulo and Belo Horizonte.

Each mosque is staffed with mullahs who offer to teach about Islam in schools, at luncheons and at other venues in the surrounding community. Guided tours in the mosque are designed to cause the curious to return for regular instruction, leading perhaps to conversion. It is a foothold. And the Koran, of course, is offered in the local language. But wouldn't *that* have a negative effect?

Arab-speaking Muslims refused for centuries to allow the Koran to be translated from Arabic.

Muslim strategists are now borrowing a leaf from Christianity's missionary methodology handbook. Over the centuries, Christian missionaries translated at least the New Testament into hundreds of languages. Muslim translators are now also rendering the Koran in dozens of key languages of the non-Muslim world.

As I have already shown, the Koran, unlike the New Testament, is its own worst detractor—but only when it is read by people who are not predisposed by intense brainwashing to accept it as inspired by God.

Arab-speaking Muslims refused for centuries to allow the Koran to be translated from Arabic. They said it was because no other language could convey the meaning so awesomely expressed in Arabic. But anyone who has read the Koran with an unfettered mind can easily guess their *real* reason. Arab Muslims were afraid to risk letting Muslim speakers of other languages discover for themselves how incredibly boring, tediously repetitive, shockingly violent and amoral the Koran actually is.

Still, Persian Muslims kept insisting that they *must* have their own translation, so—finally it was translated into Farsi, and later into Urdu for Pakistanis. Of course everyone was warned not to expect either translation to have the same overpowering effect that the original Koran has in Arabic.

Arab Muslims must have been dreading that they would hear a chorus of voices asking, "What is this? Why are we supposed to call this book 'wonderful' and 'holy' when it is neither?" Why didn't that chorus break out?

With few exceptions, the sheer boredom people felt as they tackled the Koran's frustratingly repetitive, noun-scanty, pronoun-saturated verses tended to protect it by anesthetizing the minds of foreign readers before they read far enough to realize how impoverished the text actually is! In other words, the boredom that any translation of the Koran induces tends to protect it from criticism like a shell protects a turtle! Tedium distracts many a reader after a few pages, tempting him to skip from reading to less attentive browsing. Easier to *believe* in the Koran's "greatness" than endure ennui trying to experience it.

Since languages such as Farsi and Urdu "weaken" the force of the Arabic anyway, why waste time reading it in Farsi or Urdu?

Why not just let the mullah read it in Arabic in a mosque and *imagine* the awe one would feel if only one could understand Arabic. Yet how nice, at the same time, to be able to say "We 'have' the Koran in *our* language."

So Arab queasiness about translating the Koran gave way to increased willingness to offer it, even in European languages. Once again, most Europeans left it unread or simply dismissed it as inconsequential.

Now more and more translations are fearlessly offered. Still, in mosques and madrasas everywhere, the Koran is read in Arabic. Only the sermon that follows the reading is offered in Farsi, Urdu, Indonesian or English. Still, the fact that so many translations now exist is touted as evidence of Islam's "compassionate" outreach to the world.

Infiltrate Christian Colleges and Churches
Expressly to Seduce Christian Women

A Pakistani Christian friend of mine met a young, good-looking Muslim man in London, England. Mistaking my friend for a Muslim (he knows the Koran and hadiths far better than most Muslims), the young man began bragging about a nefarious career. Claiming membership in a radical Cairo-based society called the Muslim Brotherhood, he said he was trained and funded to mingle with Christians and feign a sincere conversion to Christianity as a way to win acceptance in a church. He memorized Bible verses he knew Christians would expect him to know. He learned to pray "in Jesus' name." But why would a Muslim bother to do this?

He explained: Some of the Christians, eager to help a young convert from Islam to become established in his newfound Christian faith, would likely be well-meaning and pretty young women. Selecting one as a "hit" (preferably a pastor's daughter), the "convert" would feign romantic interest, flashing his good looks. If she responded, he would very patiently attempt to seduce her, even impregnate her, wed her and then say, "I've decided to return to Islam. Come with me!" If she refused, he would abandon her, leaving the young woman, her family, her friends and everyone else in her church fellowship in shock.

If he could not seduce her (extramaritally), he would even propose to her, wed her, impregnate her and *still* leave her.

One of the goals of this infamous ploy is to discourage Christians from trusting a *genuine* convert from Islam who might come their way. Another goal is to weaken Christian confidence in Christianity's ability to win even an occasional convert from Islam.

The career of *this* particular professed member of the Muslim Brotherhood ranged from Singapore to Sweden to London. Someone eagerly enrolled him in a Bible college in Singapore. He seduced a female fellow student. She confessed what they had done. Her repentance was genuine, and he so effectively feigned repentance that someone decided to give him a second chance by subsidizing him to fly to Sweden to enroll in another Bible college. He seduced another student there and at last was summarily dismissed, whereupon he traveled to London, where he met my Pakistani friend.

My friend warned him, "You really should not tell me these things. I am a Christian." The youth thought my friend was simply demonstrating that *he too* knew how to feign conversion to Christianity.

"Oh, you're really good!" the Muslim exclaimed, "You could really cut a swath! Have you thought of joining the Brotherhood?" A minute or so later, the Muslim realized my friend was not feigning. He blanched. He had confessed a secret Muslim strategy to a member of the house of war.

A still more subtle Muslim strategy for world conquest deserves a chapter by itself—the next chapter.

Notes

1. Maulana Muhammad Ali, *Quran* (Columbus, OH: Lahore, Inc., USA, 1998), comment 1054.
2. Donald McCurry, personal communication to author.
3. Ibn Warraq, *Why I Am Not a Muslim* (Amherst, NY: Prometheus Books, 1995), p. 355.
4. Ibid.
5. Ibid., p. 351.
6. Ibid., p. 352.
7. Ibid., p. 351.
8. Ibid.
9. "Indonesia," *ABC News*, abcnews.com (accessed December 25, 2000). Note: A search on Google.com for "Indonesia and Christmas Eve and bombs" returns about 1,200 items.

CHAPTER TWELVE

ISLAM'S PENETRATION OF WESTERN CULTURE

The Fox News Channel, on June 27, 2002, reported that foreign Muslims are pouring 13 billion dollars annually into American colleges and universities. A major part of that is, of course, tuition paid by parents for the higher education of their children. But it is not all tuition money. There is another factor.

A Presence on Western Campuses

For at least the last two decades, Islamic strategists have been seeking to influence our Western secular academic world. Backed by oil money, they begin by approaching presidents and boards of Western universities and colleges with an initial question: "Do you have a department of Islamic studies on your campus?," implying that there should of course be one. Hearing the reply, "No we don't," they next ask, "Would you like to have a really top-class one?" A dialogue similar to the following ensues:

Hearing the answer, "Yes, of course, but we do not have funding for it," the Muslim agent declares, "Funding is no problem. If your institution provides campus land, our organization will fully finance the construction of an excellent department of Islamic studies," adding, "There is one condition. If *we* fund your department of Islamic studies, naturally we must be sure that Islam is equitably represented in it. Thus you must allow us to provide professors for the new department. We guarantee qualified scholars. We may even guarantee their salaries initially—at least until tuition funds from the new department enable you to include their salaries in your regular budget. The professors we provide will even be qualified to teach certain courses in other parts of your campus at no extra expense. Isn't this an offer you can't refuse?"

If a Western secular university or college establishes *its own* department of Islamic studies and does *its own* choosing of professors who are both knowledgeable and objective, that is worthy. Some Western secular universities and colleges, however, are already accepting offers of *externally funded* departments, facultied with professors chosen by *external* funding sources from places such as Saudi Arabia or Kuwait. Granted, Muslim professors appointed by such sources may be as knowledgeable as the sun is bright, but the chance that they will teach objectively about Islam is compromised.

Western universities generally regard a department of Islamic studies as a necessity.

Muslim professors who come with the offer are expected to teach as apologists for Islam and as detractors of other religions. One of my sons took a history course taught by one such professor in Southern California. The professor cast frequent aspersions against Christianity in his lectures. Each aspersion came with an unrebutted endorsement of Islam. In a later chapter I give a rebuttal my son brought regarding one issue, much to the surprise of the Muslim professor and the rest of his class.

Welcoming a Muslim-sourced department facultied with Muslim professors constitutes a de facto academic validation of Islam as a worthy religion, the Koran as a worthy book and Mohammed as a worthy prophet. *Non-Muslim* experts on Islam will tend to not be hired if Muslims fill every teaching position in the department. Knowing that Western universities now generally regard a department of Islamic studies as a necessity, Muslim strategists find it worth the expense to be sure Muslim professors control what is taught concerning Islam.

Effects on the Entire School

Can a non-Muslim professor in other departments on the campus—assuming he or she knows disturbing facts—speak critically about Islam, the Koran and Mohammed when the institution that salaries and perhaps tenures him or her already *endorses* what he or she knows warrants criticism? Of course every university and college will protest that objectivity on its campus is never compromised for any reason. Objectivity, after all, is the lifeblood of academic reputation. Yet one is hard-pressed nowadays to find any non-Muslim professors on secular campuses who say or write anything critical of Mohammed or the Koran.

They will, of course, condemn radical Islam, implying that it has only a coincidental connection with Mohammed or the Koran. How we all wish that were true. Yet radical Islam has much more than a mere connection with Mohammed and the Koran. As I have already established from Islam's sourcebook, the Koran, radical Islam is the *real* Islam of the Koran. Moderate Islam is pseudo-Islam. As surely as those called moderates refuse to speak critically of the Koran, we may know they are living in a dream world. They are equivalent to a hypothetical 1930s German saying, "I believe Hitler is a good leader and I believe every word of his *Mein Kampf* is true, but *I am not a Nazi!*"

Moderate Muslims do not control tens of thousands of madrasas. And these Muslim madrasas are the Islamic equivalent of Hitler's Nazi youth movement, but on a vastly larger scale!

Why—when I present elements of this book in my lectures—do people who have taken university courses on Islam invariably ask, "Why was I not taught these major facts in that course I paid good money to take?"

The answer: because academic objectivity has been compromised. Ibn Warraq, in *Why I Am Not a Muslim*, chides Western academia for burying itself to the topknot in a quicksand of naiveté over Mohammed and the Koran.[1] Indeed, this trend merits scrutiny. As increasing numbers of Middle-East-appointed Muslim scholars blend into Western academia, the quicksand's suction will only increase.

Islam in the Social Science Classroom

We must not overlook the fact that humanistic social science professors in Western academia from Moscow to Melbourne have, for decades, been prone not only to smile indulgently upon Islam but also to attack Christianity. Read *Christianity on Trial: Arguments Against Anti-Religious Bigotry* by Vincent Carroll and David Shiflett[2] or my own, "Scholars with Strange Theories," a chapter in *Eternity in Their Hearts*,[3] for a study of anti-Christian antagonism in academia and its theoretical foundations.

A Christian student at Washington State University once told me that his humanistic anthropology professor warned him, "Young man, I am going to do everything I can in this semester to destroy your faith in Christianity!"

And now, strangely, that mind-set that will not tolerate Christianity is so *open* to Islam!

"What could I have said?" the bewildered young Christian asked. I replied, "Are there students in that class who follow other religions?"

"Yes," he said. "As a matter of fact, a Hindu, a Muslim and a Buddhist attend as well."

"Has he warned them that he intends to attack *their* beliefs?"

"No, he hasn't."

"Then you should question his objectivity in singling out *just* Christianity for attack, when in fact as a secular humanist he dislikes all religions, except as objects for anthropological study, of course."

At this point I must offer a generalization. By definition, every generalization has exceptions. It is valid to generalize, as long as one acknowledges that there will be exceptions. Here is my generalization: For more than a century, social science departments in almost every secular college and university in the Western world have been, at least partially, exploited as tax-funded anti-Christian madrasas for secular humanism.

And how does *that* square with separation of religion and state?

A Parable for These Modern Times

Following my generalization, I offer a parable: A certain farmer in a faraway land had a mongoose, some chickens and a few goats. The chickens provided him with eggs and the goats with milk. "But this mongoose," he said one day, "what does it do for me? Sometimes it scampers on the roof at night, waking me. Occasionally it consumes an egg from a hen's nest, depriving me. Besides that, I'm allergic to its fur."

Finally he decided he did not like his mongoose, and he killed it.

Later he noticed that not only an occasional egg, but an occasional chicken was missing, and then an occasional goat! At last the farmer discovered the problem: His mongoose had been

> **Secular humanists, agnostics and atheists have assumed that if they could rid their world of Christianity, no other religion would take its place. Wrong assumption!**

keeping pythons away. Without the mongoose, pythons slithered in and fed on the farmer's eggs. Growing larger feeding on eggs, they soon fed on his chickens. Growing larger feeding on chickens, they were soon able to swallow his goats.

"O mongoose! Mongoose!" the farmer cried, "If only I could have you back! I would not shout at you when you scamper on my roof. You wouldn't have to take an occasional egg for your services—I would *give* you an egg a day! I would still be allergic to your fur, but better a sneeze now and then than these pythons!

"Like a fool I killed my mongoose to save a few eggs," the farmer moaned, "only to lose my eggs *and* my hens *and* my goats to pythons."

The point: Secular humanists, agnostics and atheists have always assumed that if they could rid their world of this nuisance called Christianity, no other religion would rush in to take its place. Wrong assumption! Mankind as a species comes with an instinct for religion. Secular humanists, agnostics and atheists may manage to anesthetize their inbuilt religious instinct, but a majority of mankind still chooses religion. If people cannot have one religion, a majority will eventually turn to another.

Relentless areligious social science academics, exploiting their status as teachers of one generation after another, have indeed ridiculed, discredited and *weakened* Christianity—especially in Europe, Canada and Australia. Cathedrals are largely empty (not that building architectural wonders was *ever* a wise use of Christian money!). Church services are echoey for lack of worshipers.

But the secularist educators' victory is Pyrrhian. They have shot themselves in both feet; the pain just hasn't reached their brains yet. They have freely given Islam opportunity to rush in and begin replacing Christianity where they have weakened it. We now live in a day where Muslim oil money is purchasing thousands of empty European, Canadian and American churches and changing them to mosques. Vital Christianity could have had a mongoose effect, given a better chance. But now the supremacist Muslim python is in the henhouse and is even eyeing the goat pen of secularist antireligionism and its academic freedoms.

Advice to Secularists

I have good advice for secularists who claim they are allergic to Christianity: Better to tolerate a religion that resembles an occasionally irritating mongoose than to kill the mongoose and by so doing unwittingly welcome the python; i.e., an extremist religion that will avidly *crush* your freedom to be a secular humanist, an agnostic or an atheist!

In an Islam-dominated world, try ridiculing Islam in your classroom the way you ridicule Christianity. Under Sharia law, how quickly your head will roll in a gutter! To put it another way, not only your eggs, but even your hens and goats—your academic freedom, your *rights*—will vanish down that other religion's throat.

How much does true Islam tolerate secular humanism, agnosticism or atheism? The answer: even less than it tolerates apostasy! And apostasy has always been a capital offense in the Koran and in the hadiths. Apostasy automatically incurs a death penalty in strict Muslim nations such as Saudi Arabia and Pakistan.

Mankind being mankind, there always will be a religion near you. You, as professors, have some influence as to which religion will continue to be there. Christianity—which, at least in this age, fully acknowledges your freedom to oppose it—has been there, but you have weakened its ability to protect your right to continue opposing it and other religions.

Among the world's religions, Christianity (*not* pseudo-Christianity and not even Buddhism with its commendable practice of nonviolence) is ethically *most opposite* to Islam and, as an evangelizing religion, it is the one with the keenest mettle to take Islam on in a peaceful ideological struggle—a so-welcome departure from pseudo-Christianity's crusades and inquisitions of the past. Christianity is thus best able to provide a mongoose effect vis-à-vis Islam for you secularists, if given a fair chance.

I know that humanists, agnostics and atheists who read this may disagree. But can you afford to wait to see me proved wrong?

It is time for people like you and people like me—remembering our differences—to consult together for our mutual self-preservation.

An Elementary Affront

Islam is not only entrenching itself securely in Western institutions of *higher* education. It is even invading Western academia at elementary school levels. Dr. James L. Garlow, in *A Christian's Response to Islam,* warns:

> In Byron, California, seventh-grade students are made to dress up as Muslims, read the Koran, and conduct a "holy war" or *jihad* using a dice game in a state-mandated curriculum which does not offer the same privilege to the Christian faith. The New York City public schools administration now allows Muslim children to be excused from classes to go to a state-funded classroom for their daily prayers. Christian children are forbidden to pray or conduct Bible studies in the same schools. In Massachusetts, the governor [now former] has expressed interest in introducing Muslim teaching into the state's school curriculum.[4]

In Byron, I should note, the school claims that its startlingly pro-Islamic class activities followed state guidelines—a totally unreassuring statement if there ever was one! It also claims the class activities in question were voluntary, but incensed parents differ and have filed a lawsuit.

Meanwhile, across the Atlantic, naive European educators who thought they could assimilate Muslims into European culture, are now discovering that Islam is determined to assimilate Europeans to Islam. Muslims in Europe are now *demanding* that Islam be taught in public schools as superior to every other religion.

AN ASSAULT WITHIN THE CHURCH

Social science academians are not alone in assaulting biblical Christianity relentlessly. Liberal theologians within the Church contribute tragically to the *pseudoization* of Christianity—this time from the Protestant side—by teaching specious theories from German higher criticism.[5] Muslim apologists eagerly appropriate liberal attacks on the New Testament and exploit them for Islamic propaganda.

It saves Muslims so much work! They don't have to dig to devise anti-New Testament arguments. For example, the Jesus Seminar, a group of liberal theologians investigating the claims of Jesus, published a report that unwittingly offers Muslims ready-to-heat-and-serve anti-New Testament stratagems, however specious, on a platter.

Weakening the faith of Lutheran Christians especially, German higher critics first diminished Lutheranism's ability to have a mongoose effect against Nazism in the 1930s. Now they are rendering several mainline denominations—in Europe especially—largely impotent vis-à-vis Islam.

ISLAM AND HOLLYWOOD

What about Islam's long-range plans for Hollywood?

Western cinema and television do produce a few equitable depictions of Christianity. *Chariots of Fire*, *The Sound of Music* and *Shadowlands* are prime examples. Still, a sizable majority of films and television programs are grossly violent, slutty or hideously occult. Muslims, Hindus and Buddhists across the world tend to react vehemently against such products, even though they may sit down and view them. Radical Muslims especially blame Christianity for Western media's seductiveness, saying in so many words, "See how *Christian America* is corrupting us!"

One of Islam's ultimate goals is to reverse what it perceives as Christianity's and Judaism's failures to *forcibly* prevent prurient productions in Western media. Islam does not understand Judeo-Christianity's patience in seeking to overcome evil via charisma and example. Radical Islam's preference will be to unleash an immediate, heavy-handed, even brutal *destruction* of corrupting media.

Islam does not understand Judeo-Christianity's patience in seeking to overcome evil via charisma and example.

Media people, take note. You too should give thought *now* as to how you may plan to avoid excessive censorship in an Islam-dominated world—a world that hypothetically could exist a few decades from now. First, clean up your own act voluntarily, because Islam *hates* your product. Second, give thought to Christianity—the religion many of you prefer to disdain, but that is ethically most opposite to Islam—as something that, given a little help, is your best hope for a positive protective mongoose effect, affording you some protection.

You won't even need to say "Thank you."

Rapid Assimilation

Dick Morris, former advisor to President Clinton, in recent speeches and writings, says that Muslim immigrant percentages in the population of various European nations range from 10 to 20 percent—and they are rising! European governments, he warns, hesitate to support America's war against terrorism, especially on Arab soil, for fear of the havoc radical Muslims in their own societies will wreak in retaliation.

Morris further warns that America, with the passage of time, will have to go it alone.[6] But Muslim immigrant percentages are rising here too. Like the Borg in Star Trek, dominance-achieving supremacist Islam says to all non-Muslims, "You will be assimilated."

The python is already slithering from the henhouse into the goat pen. A different kind of war is here, on our soil. It is in our suburbs, in our schools, in our colleges, in our businesses. Appropriate countermeasures must be taken. We must determine what are appropriate countermeasures. Any definition of pluralism that negates any and all countermeasures must be abandoned. During the Cold War, were we interested in pluralistic accommodations for communism? Of course not. But radical Islam is just as much and politically even more a threat to our freedoms as communism ever was.

Notes

1. Ibn Warraq, *Why I Am Not a Muslim* (Amherst, NY: Prometheus Books, 1995), pp. 236-237.
2. Vincent Carroll and David Shiflett, *Christianity on Trial: Arguments Against Anti-Religious Bigotry* (San Francisco, CA: Encounter Books, 2002).
3. Don Richardson, "Scholars with Strange Theories" in *Eternity in Their Hearts* (Ventura, CA: Regal Books, 1981), pp. 133-150.
4. James Garlow, *A Christian's Response to Islam* (Tulsa, OK: River Oak Publishing, 2002), n.p.
5. For more on this subject, see my book *Eternity in Their Hearts* (Ventura, CA: Regal Books, 1981).
6. Dick Morris makes frequent appearances on Fox News and C-SPAN and has written several best-selling books.

CHAPTER THIRTEEN

A TWENTY-FIRST CENTURY PLAGUE OF LOCUSTS?

Imagine if Western governments—the United States, Canada, England, Germany and the others—allowed a cult far more sinister and better funded than the Ku Klux Klan or the Aryan Nation to enroll tens of millions of male students in thousands of private schools. The schools are staffed by teachers intent upon brainwashing the students by forcing them to memorize hundreds of key verses from a professedly holy book as well as from commentaries on the same. Imagine that many of the verses and commentaries quoted teach students to hate Muslims and to be prepared even to *die* while killing Muslims as a service for God.

Imagine such teaching continuing year after year.

Imagine those tens of millions of boys, as they become young men, being warned just as incessantly that if they desert, if they refuse to fight or if they refuse to support those who do fight for God, He will punish them with utter torment in the fires of hell forever.

Imagine millions of these young enrollees entering puberty. Their sexual hormones are fully activated, but they are scarcely allowed to see, let alone mingle, with members of the opposite sex. Instead they must memorize still *more* verses from the professed holy book, supplemented again by commentaries, all of which promise that if they do fight in God's holy war—and especially if they *die* a martyr's death in that war—a *very* special award awaits them. Instead of waiting who knows how long to learn if God deigns to welcome them to paradise, they will be ushered in at once! And who will they find waiting there to welcome them? Departed relatives who have gone before? That supposed holy book they now know so well describes paradise repeatedly, but not once does it mention loved ones reunited in heaven.

No! The second set of verses and commentary so diligently memorized promises these tens of millions of young males entering the full strength of puberty that God offers them something very opposite to eternal torment in hell. They will have instead a host of beautiful young virgins to have sex with for eternity. What could be a more cruel enticement for teenage boys, especially when it is contrasted with the antithetical alternative—torment in hell? Clearly this multimillion-member international student body would be trained for one thing only:

relentless suicidal terrorism. It would resemble a human equivalent of a Tolkienian army of Auks hell-bent for war.

All the while, relatively little time is spent on reading, writing and arithmetic and *none* on teaching computer skills. Graduates are unqualified for preferred jobs—*by design!* No one ever wanted the students to qualify for preferred jobs, except perhaps the students and their poor duped parents.

Does this mean the best of the graduates will be unemployed? No fear! Guess who are waiting to guarantee them, not a salary so much, but food, shelter, friendship and an opportunity to serve God? Terrorist recruiters.

Surely not even Edgar Allen Poe or Stephen King could concoct in fiction a more calculatedly vicious brainwashing industry. By now you readers are pleading, *Please assure me that nothing resembling the above horrible nightmare exists anywhere in the world and never will!*

It does exist! What Western democratic governments would never permit against Muslims, dozens of Islamic governments are allowing and condoning, if not promoting against non-Muslims. Hitler's Nazi youth movement was not nearly so nefarious, and it influenced a mere one-thousandth as many youth as are being trained in Muslim madrasas. Supremacist Islam is preparing a new holocaust for the non-Muslim world in the form of tens of millions of brainwashed madrasa graduates. They are being readied to blight our Earth like a swarm of locusts of biblical proportions.

How are we to prepare ourselves?

THE PROMOTIONAL ROLE OF PALESTINIAN MEDIA

Occasionally what is taught conspiratorially behind madrasa walls spills out through Muslim media. IMRA—an acrostic for

Independent Media Review Analysis—reported that Yasser Arafat's Palestinian Broadcasting Corporation, on June 27, 2002, aired a video that portrays the Islamic view of the reward that awaits a Muslim martyr immediately after death.

In the video, a Muslim man walking with his wife frowns when he sees a group of Israeli soldiers. In an apparent vision, he sees a bevy of stunningly beautiful heavenly girls beckoning to him as they emerge from a mist. He understands their invitation and does something that causes the Israeli soldiers to kill him. His wife, shown in her mid-30s, weeps bitterly over her husband's body. He, however, has no need to miss her. The video shows him beaming happily as the lovely women, younger and more beautiful than his wife, caressingly lead him away to an

> **One would hope that better-educated Muslims are endeavoring to oppose the supremacist madness.**

endless tryst in the mist. Fade to black.

No Hitler, Mussolini or Stalin ever thought of *that* way of motivating their troops.

One would hope that better-educated Muslims are endeavoring to oppose the supremacist madness taught in such a production and in so many madrasas. But a June 28, 2002, analysis by Harold Evans—former president of Random House Publishing, former editorial director of *Atlantic Monthly* and author of *The American Century*—quotes various Middle-Eastern Muslim intellectuals as endorsing the madness. Evans cites Dr. Adel Sadeq, chairman of the Arab Psychiatrists Association and professor of psychiatry at Cairo's Ein Shams University, as saying:

A certain Muslim website invites questions about any aspect of Islam. Mullahs choose several questions a day and answer them. One questioner asked if the wives of Muslim men, arriving in paradise, would feel understandably jealous, knowing that their husbands were having sex with houris (virgins) in heaven. A mullah responded with a quote from a hadith to the effect that Aisha, one of Mohammed's wives, asked Mohammed that very question. According to the mullah's hadithic reference, Mohammed replied that there could be no jealousy in paradise. He also assured Aisha that she need not worry, because in paradise she would be more beautiful than in this life, enabling her to compete well with the houris for his attention.

As a professional psychiatrist, I say that the height of bliss [for a suicide bomber] comes at the end of the countdown . . . four, three, two, one. When the martyr reaches *one* and he explodes, he has a sense of himself flying, because he knows for certain that he is not dead. It is a transition to another, more beautiful world. No one in the Western world sacrifices his life for his homeland. If his homeland is drowning [sic], he is the first to jump ship. In our culture it is different. . . . This is the only Arab weapon. . . . Anyone who says otherwise is a conspirator.[1]

Evans responds, "Next patient, please!"

He also avers that the European Community is giving millions of dollars to Arafat's Palestinian Liberation Authority. Part of that trove finances the kind of fanatical madrasa instruction that teaches young Palestinians to blow themselves up, killing as many Israelis as possible in the process.

Will it stop with warring against Israelis? Israelis defend as best they can, but how will *we* defend ourselves against possible future fanatics vying with each other for opportunities to kill us, all the while hoping to be killed by us as a way of paying the only sure-to-be-accepted entry fee into Allah's great heavenly brothel?

Note

1. Harold Evans, "The Anti-Semitic Lies That Threaten All of Us," *Times of London* (June 28, 2002), condensed from a speech given by Evans at the Index on Censorship conference.

CHAPTER FOURTEEN

EUROPE: AN AUTO-GENOCIDING CONTINENT

Dick Morris, former advisor to President Bill Clinton, is now warning America in speeches and in a book, *Power Plays: Win or Lose—How History's Great Political Leaders Play the Game*, that Islam's permeation of and threatening presence in Western Europe intimidates many of America's allies from fully endorsing, for example, an American assault on terrorism in Muslim nations. In a C-SPAN 2 cable television broadcast aired on June

9, 2002, Morris opined that cities such as London and Paris are safe from major terrorist attacks because key terrorists live there.[1] That could change, however, if England, France or Germany were to encourage America to extend its war against terrorism, especially in the Middle East.

Columnist Patrick Buchanan, a former presidential speech-writer for President Ronald Reagan and two-time presidential candidate, explains why Muslim immigration into Western Europe can only soar in the near future. Buchanan writes that he could not find, in a recent quest,

> a single European nation, save Muslim Albania, with a birth rate to enable it to survive in its present form through mid-century. The United Nations projects Europe will lose 124 million people by 2050. . . . Some European nations already report more burials than births. Not since the Black Plague has Europe seen a population collapse like this. . . . Just to maintain the current 4.8-to-1 ratio of working-age population (ages 15-64) to seniors (65 and above), Europe must import 1.4 billion people by 2050.[2]

Is Europe's accelerating population collapse due to myriad abortions only, or is it also because a critical mass of Europeans now find parenting to be impractical, since both spouses must work due to Europe's high income taxes? Buchanan's article does not explain. He moves to his next point:

> Where will [the 1.4 billion needed immigrants] come from? North Africa, the Middle East and the ex-colonies of the old empires. . . . Moroccan[s] . . . are returning to Spanish towns their Moorish ancestors were expelled from in 1492. Islam has begun to reconquer Europe. . . .

As Christian churches of Europe empty out, mosques are filling up. There are 2,000 mosques in Germany and 5 million Muslims in France. [Plus, each year] an estimated half million illegals [enter Europe].[3]

Buchanan cites omens of a grim future for Europe:

Race riots erupted in the British Midland towns of Bradford, Burnley, Oldham and Leeds. In Paris, Algerian toughs stormed a soccer field during a game with France, chanting Osama bin Laden's name as terrified Parisians locked themselves in skyboxes.[4]

Dick Morris voiced another warning in his C-SPAN 2 address: Islam's growing strength in Western Europe, he claims, is contributing to a renewal of European *anti-Semitism*.[5] One wonders if Morris had in mind Jeff Jacoby's article, "The Canary In Europe's Mine," that appeared in the *Boston Globe* on April 28, 2002. Jacoby wrote:

The rocks have been lifted all over Europe and the snakes of Jew-hatred are slithering free. In Belgium, thugs beat up the chief rabbi, kicking him in the face. . . . Two synagogues in Brussels were fire-bombed; a third, in Charleroi, was sprayed with automatic weapons fire. . . . A Jewish Yeshiva student reading the Psalms [on a London bus] was stabbed 27 times. . . . In Germany, thousands of neo-Nazis marched near a synagogue on the Sabbath. . . . But nowhere have the flames of anti-Semitism burned more furiously than in France. In Lyon, a [burning] car was rammed into a synagogue. In Montpellier, the Jewish religious center was firebombed; so were synagogues in Strasbourg and Marseille; so was a Jewish school in Creteil. A Jewish sportsclub in Toulouse was attacked with Molotov cocktails.[6]

After describing at least a dozen more unconscionable villainies, Jacoby concludes:

> Anti-Semitism . . . has been a part of European society since time immemorial [except] in the aftermath of the Holocaust. . . . [Once again] Europe is reverting to type. To be sure, some Europeans are shocked. But the more common reaction is complacency . . . a grievous mistake. Violence [aimed today] at Jews, tomorrow will be aimed at . . . Christians.[7]

Jacoby makes no mention of violent Muslims perpetrating the above assaults. If neo-Nazis and skinheads are willing to do the dirty work, why should violent Muslims soil their hands? But the hatred of Jews and of Israel that neo-Nazis, skinheads and violent Muslims share makes the possibility of *collusion* between them a danger for which law enforcers should prepare.

Western Europe is a wayward Titanic tragically impaled upon an iceberg: supremacist Islam.

Anti-semitism underlies Europe like a black coal seam: thin here, thick there; deep here, surfacing there. Nazis strip-mined the seam massively in 1930s' Germany. Communists have been steam-shoveling it to the surface across Eastern Europe for almost a century. Radical Muslims will surely be tempted to set underground fires burning in that seam today.

Western Europe is a wayward Titanic tragically impaled upon an iceberg: supremacist Islam. Neither Morris nor Buchanan suggest that America should somehow alter course for a rescue attempt. How does so young a country help an older society that sees itself as a capstone on the pyramid of wisdom? Help from America, to be accepted by Europe, would have to be disguised with consummate subtlety. Perhaps that much finesse is beyond us. But if we find a way to offer help that Europe will accept, let's help. The trouble is this: The same iceberg is puncturing the hull of our own ship of state.

Notes

1. Dick Morris, "Booknotes: Power Plays," C-Span 2, June 9, 2002.
2. Patrick Buchanan, "Forum," *USA Today*, March 5, 2002, n.p.
3. Ibid.
4. Ibid.
5. Dick Morris, "Booknotes: Power Plays," C-Span 2, June 9, 2002.
6. Jeff Jacoby, "The Canary In Europe's Mine," *Boston Globe*, April 28, 2002, n.p.
7. Ibid.

CHAPTER FIFTEEN

LOUIS FARRAKHAN, ISLAM AND SLAVERY

Several years ago CNN's Larry King interviewed Louis Farrakhan, head of the Nation of Islam—a uniquely American and heretical cultic offshoot from mainstream Islam. King asked Farrakhan why he advises Afro-Americans to spurn Christianity and embrace Islam.

Farrakhan said Christianity is the religion of those who enslaved black Africans. Conversely, as a religion that has long championed the rights of the black race, Islam deserves the allegiance of black Afro-Americans.[1]

Larry King had not done adequate homework for an interview with Farrakhan. He failed to probe Farrakhan with questions that could have made the interview livelier, not to mention much more relevant.

Farrakhan, said to be funded in part by oil money from Libya and the Sudan, gives Muslim leaders worldwide cause to hope that Islam will triumph over Christianity and secularism in America.[2] Headlines in the Arab world announce that large numbers of black Americans have already converted to Islam, and millions more are weighing their decision. Descendants of the very Africans that Christian slavers took to America, they assert, have by Allah's mercy become a means of drawing America at last to Islam.

The king of Saudi Arabia, if he holds to the standard Koranic definition of a Muslim, could hardly regard Farrakhan as much more than a heretic. Yet he endorses him. Inviting Farrakhan to a palace deep in the desert heartland of Islam, the Saudi king honored him with a sizable financial reward for his usefulness in providing a beachhead for Islam in America.

If Islam ever dominates America, Louis Farrakhan types will be brushed aside. They may even be branded as heretics for tampering with Muslim doctrine. For example, Islam rejects the Nation of Islam's definition of Satan as none other than the entire white race.

The Slavery Factor

At the time of the Larry King interview one of my sons was taking a course in African history at a Southern California university. The professor, a Muslim from Kenya, used the classroom to level the same charge Farrakhan had made on King's nationwide program, abasing Christianity for abetting slavery and honoring Islam for supposedly opposing enslavement.

Had the professor also heard King's interview with Farrakhan? Did King's failure to probe Farrakhan's assertion cue the Kenyan to rote what Farrakhan had said? Perhaps.

My son said to me, "As the only Christian in the class, I was embarrassed. I didn't know what to say. Was he right?"

Indeed some black pastors across America have also been stymied when an occasional black youth leaves the Church to join Farrakhan. Advantaged with oil money, the Nation of Islam often surpasses the efforts of Christians in inner-city development projects and in the reclamation of black prison inmates from a life of crime. The Nation of Islam hired a Muslim lawyer and paid the legal expenses of the black youths accused of beating Reginald Denny almost to death during riots in Los Angeles that followed the Rodney King trial verdict.

Millions of black Afro-Americans regard Abraham Lincoln, a Christian, as a deliverer (however imperfect) of their enslaved forebears—a virtual *saint!* Farrakhan is not pleased. Speaking at the Million Man March in Washington, D.C., Farrakhan—ever smiling amid his clutch of ever-frowning bodyguards—dismissed Lincoln as "the man who allegedly freed us."[3] How should Christians, especially black pastors, respond?

The Truth About Slavery's Roots

For a start, I directed my son to turn to "slavery—the history of" in virtually any encyclopedia. There we learn that the word "slave" in English derives from Slav.[4] The Romans, in a day when slavery was worldwide, captured Slavs in Eastern Europe and sold them as slaves throughout the Roman Empire. No one had yet proven the feasibility of caravaning the vast Sahara desert en masse to capture *black* slaves in distant, mysterious sub-Saharan Africa.

Once Islam had spread across North Africa in the 600s, however, Muslim slavers in the 700s tested caravan routes across the Sahara. They came to areas now called Cameroon, Nigeria, Benin, Togo, Ghana and Burkina Faso. There they found African tribes already raiding each other for slaves. The only thing Muslim slavers had to do was arm and equip the *northernmost* black tribes—Hausas, Fulanis, Kolofs and others—with swords, crossbows, manacles and chains, giving them both military and slave-grabbing advantage over more southerly tribes.

Of course, Muslims trained their protege accomplices to steal slaves only from more southerly tribes, not from each other. Muslims added a profit motive to an already cruel custom. Instead of taking fewer slaves for their own convenience, northern sub-Saharans began capturing enormous numbers of their southern neighbors to be sold away to distant North Africa.

By trial and error, Muslim slavers found that if large numbers of slaves were force-marched northward across 1,200 miles or more of Sahara sand, enough would survive to guarantee a profit when they were sold in North African slave bazaars. Slavers from Muslim Libya, Morocco, Algeria, Tunisia and Egypt began launching thousands of trans-Saharan caravans. The wholesale enslavement of the black race was under way. Europeans would not get into the act until the 1600s—*by finally following the example that their North African Muslim neighbors had been virtually taunting them with for 900 years.*

Other Muslim slavers avoided arduous trans-Saharan treks. Sailing comfortably down the coast of East Africa, they built a slave-collecting base on Zanzibar Island. They similarly armed and equipped coastal black tribes adjacent to Zanzibar and trained them to raid hapless interior tribes for slaves, instead of each other.

Muslim slavers soon brought mullahs to teach Islam. But the mullahs fulfilled their mission only among tribes accomplished with Muslims as slave gatherers. Areas ravaged by Muslim-induced slave raids were war zones where Muslim missionaries dared not reside. Thus Islam won black converts only along the 4,000-mile-long southern fringe of the Sahara from Senegal to Somalia (the widest part of Africa) and on a crescent of coastline facing Zanzibar.

Islam's Advantage in Time

In the meantime, lacking the zeal that marked their apostolic-age beginnings, Christians—cloistered in Europe—unwittingly gave Islam a 1,000-year head start in sub-Saharan Africa. That should have given Islam an advantage in sub-Saharan Africa that no amount of subsequent Christian missionary labor could ever overtake. Yet Muslim mullahs, by siding with Muslim slavers instead of with the slavers' black African victims, forfeited the boon of that 1,000-year head start.

Had mullahs opposed slavery instead of condoning it, they could have ranged freely from Timbuktu almost to Cape Town, opening mosques and establishing Islamic schools in the region. In short, they could have Islamicized *all of Africa*, not just a fringe above and below the Sahara and on the coast of Zanzibar. Christian missionaries, arriving belatedly in the early 1800s, would have found church planting in Zimbabwe and Zululand as difficult as planting churches in Algeria today.

Alas, Islam's mullahs in black Africa had a problem: The Koran did not authorize them to oppose slavery. How could they oppose what the Koran endorses?

The Koran itself was on the side of the slavers because Mohammed himself was a slaver! That was a problem New Testament-guided Christian missionaries would not have—if only some would just show up! When a handful finally arrived, they were soon followed by more and eventually by throngs.

Muslims during that millennium of slaving did not dream that in a later century a budding new branch of European Christianity would rediscover the New Testament as a message from God to be dispensed to the whole world. That fresh new force would also rediscover the New Testament way to communicate biblical truth—a way that spurns political help and even the military protection of secular government in favor of gentle charisma, consistent example and reasoned persuasion.

When I say new branch, I do *not* refer to the Protestant Reformation as a whole. I refer only to the Anabaptist wing of the Protestant Reformation, organized in Augsburg, Germany, in 1527. It began by immediately sending missionaries across Central Europe, but it was planning on reaching the world.

Islam's mullahs in black Africa had a problem: The Koran did not authorize them to oppose slavery.

A Short History of Christian Mission

The main part of the Reformation—apart from some token missionary activity here and there—was born missionless, like a baby with a missing arm, from the minds of men like Martin Luther, John Calvin and Ulrich Zwingli. Not only so, mainstream Protestants persecuted and even killed the only Protestants who were doing mission work—their Anabaptist brothers and sisters.

Some mainstream Protestants even butchered Jews who refused to convert. They were guilty of what ought to be called a Protestant inquisition. Anabaptists who survived their predations were too few to resume the missionary calling they saw as their destiny. Not until the mid 1800s were Anabaptists finally free to spread their wings worldwide. By then, most Anabaptists were called Mennonites.

Mainstream Protestants chose to waste the first two centuries of the post-Reformation era before deigning to credit Anabaptists with being right about at least one thing—mission! Before that brighter era dawned, however, a *second* Anabaptist-like movement birthed under and spread out from the dubious shelter of a Protestantism that was still hostile to missions.

It was the Moravian movement, born near Dresden, Germany, in 1722. This was the movement that would finally cut a Christian trail to sub-Saharan Africa. At last someone would bring the freeing love of Jesus to tens of millions of Africans afflicted by 1,000 years of Muslim slaving. At last people who see all people as "created in the likeness of God" would be there. Moravians led the way!

Jailhouse Evangelism

Wherever Moravian missionaries went, they identified first with slaves, if any were present. When European slaveholders in a Caribbean island called Saint Thomas imprisoned Moravians for fraternizing with their slaves, each Sunday hundreds of slaves waited until their owners carriaged off to church. Then they rushed to the prison to hear the Moravians preach from between the bars on the jailhouse windows. Eight hundred slaves in Saint Thomas became devout, hymn-singing Christians.

Where was the ideal church in Saint Thomas—under the steeples or at the jailhouse?

The more the Moravian example was discussed, the more other people were helped at last to see slave owning as *shameful*—a big first step toward abolition.

Moravians were also the first body since New Testament days to declare categorically that Christians must never resent, let alone harm, Jews for refusing to acknowledge Jesus as Messiah. Conversion compelled is no conversion at all.

Loving witness with winsome persuasion is the only approach to leading people to Jesus, no matter how sadly or how often the method may fail.

Extending the Missionary Effort

Moravian missionaries learned indigenous languages from Greenland to Cape Town. They taught slaves to read, provided for widows and orphans, nursed the sick and translated for others the Scriptures they so thoroughly loved and aspired to live by. Historian Paul E. Pierson comments: "[The Moravians] were not to seek glory for themselves. The missionary was to be content to suffer, die and be forgotten."[5]

Just as important as their own labors was the inspiration Moravians so profoundly ignited in others. Through their influence, John and Charles Wesley discovered the meaning of true conversion, and the Methodist movement was launched worldwide. In the 1790s, William Carey, an English Baptist, citing the Moravian example, saw dozens of disinterested pastors become avid supporters of his mission to India.

As zeal for missions caught on in continental Europe, even mainstream Protestant churches that once persecuted Anabaptist missionaries initially and later, to a lesser degree, even the Moravians, began forming their mission agencies, too. The baby born with a missing arm was growing one!

Expansion to Sub-Saharan Africa

And so they came! Missionaries began arriving in sub-Saharan Africa at last—woefully late but oh so zealous! Probably the first was Moravian Georg Schmidt, who began his work on Africa's southernmost tip in 1738. In 1787, anti-slavery Christians in London arranged for 411 slaves to be freed, educated and sent back to West Africa to establish a haven and a college for thousands of other soon-to-be-released slaves at Freetown, in what is now Sierra Leone.

Following Freetown's example, other communities for freed slaves opened at Abeokuta and Badagry, both in Nigeria. As fast as British warships forcibly rescued captive Africans from Portuguese and Spanish slave ships on the open Atlantic, they delivered them to these three Christian-sponsored African havens.

In addition, Robert Moffat opposed slavery from South Africa to Bechuana, beginning in 1816. Other missionaries reached Ethiopia in 1830. Mary Slessor opposed slavery in Calabar, beginning in the 1840s, as did David Livingston in East Africa in the 1850s.

Soon Christian missionaries were actively opposing both European and Muslim slave raiding almost everywhere in sub-Saharan Africa. Not only so, but they refused to accept donations for the support of their work from anyone back home who was a slave owner!

By the year 1900, approximately 4 million sub-Saharan Africans were Christians. By then, European slave trading was long gone. Muslim slave trading receded gradually northward, but still persists adamantly *even today* among both pagan and Muslim Hausas, Fulanis, Arabs, Libyans and Somalis.

Christian missionaries opposed both European and Muslim slave raiding in sub-Saharan Africa.

That is not all: 4 million African Christians in 1900 became more than 300 million by the year 2000.

Consider that all 300 million Christians in sub-Saharan Africa would likely be Muslims today had not the Koran itself prevented Muslim mullahs from opposing Islam's slave trade in Africa. Thus did Islam *waste* the 1,000-year head start Christianity allowed it to have in black Africa.

SLAVERY TODAY

Slavery was not declared illegal in Saudi Arabia, mainstay of Muslim purity, until 1965, and then only because Saudis grew weary of being chided as barbarian by a host of democratic nations. Muslim Sudan did not make slavery illegal until 1991, but still permits it. Abundant media reports confirm that black slaves from the southern Sudan are still being bought and sold today through Arab northern Sudan into Libya. *Reader's Digest*, in March 1996, published an article titled "Slavery's Shameful Return to Africa." Actually, slavery never left Muslim North Africa. A better title for the *Reader's Digest* article would have been "Islam's Shameful Perpetuation of Slavery in Africa."

Here is a quote from an *Economist* article, "The Flourishing Business of Slavery":

> London [sic; Zurich, Switzerland-based] based Christian Solidarity International has ransomed 20 Sudanese slaves. [Yet] the Sudanese government flatly denies that slavery exists there. It is lying. Evidence from human rights organizations, exiles, traders and former slaves is overwhelming. Louis Farrakhan, occasional guest of the Libyan and Sudanese governments, has rebuffed assertions of slavery in Sudan as Zionist claptrap. . . . He challenged journalists to go to Sudan and find it. Two reporters from the *Baltimore Sun* did just that and published their findings . . . sparking a lively debate among . . . black Muslims in particular as to how they should respond to the plight of enslaved black Africans.[6]

Why debate? The first and best response is simply to forsake Islam! If two or three very prominent black male Muslims, looking at these shameful facts, would summarily and publicly renounce Islam—even if over the slavery issue alone—surely millions of other Muslim men who are people of conscience will emulate them. If any kind of protest can ever give Islam sufficient incentive to purge present-day slavery from a score or more of Islamic nations, that might do it!

I said *male* Muslims because protests by Muslim women will be summarily disregarded. If protesting Muslim women are married to Muslims who disapprove of their protests, their husbands have the option of following Mohammed's advice in verse 4:34 (4:38, some versions): **"As for [disobedient wives] beat them" (Koran,** *Dawood, Arberry and Rodwell*). M. M. Ali and M. Z. Khan prefer to obscure the physical abuse aspect from modern eyes with **"chastise them."**

Female Protesters?

If a Muslim man is thoroughly angry with a wife who protests what the Koran permits, he has only to divorce her by saying to her three times, "I divorce you." Then he may marry another woman in her place.[7]

But of course, embarrassingly, even if all Islamic nations end slavery—yielding to whatever kind of incentive—slavery will still forever be endorsed in that stubbornly immutable Koran.

If not even *one* prominent Muslim, seeing the abundant evidence that links Islam with present-day slavery, has the courage to do what should be done, what does *that* reveal about Islam's effect upon human conscience?

Many Muslims will brand dissenters as apostates. But in the eyes of every slave who may be freed through their protest—and in the eyes of those they may spare from ever being enslaved—they will be esteemed as virtual apostles. History will remember them along with abolitionist giants such as William Wilberforce and Abraham Lincoln. But where *are* the new generation abolitionists in the camp of Islam?

Descendants of Slaves

Here is another perspective on slavery that Mr. Farrakhan will perhaps wish could be kept hidden. For every African brought as a slave to the United States, many more were abducted to Muslim North Africa, Arabia and the Middle East. One would expect, then, to find many times as many descendants of slaves living today in North Africa, Arabia and the Middle East as are found in America.

Some 30 million descendants of African slaves reside in America today. Where, then, are the perhaps 300 million descendants of African slaves that should be residing across North Africa, the Middle East and Arabia today? Why are they nowhere to be seen?

This is where encyclopedias, *National Geographic* magazine and other media err or simply hide a truth well-known to black elders across sub-Saharan Africa.

The grim horror is that Muslim slavers customarily castrated black males that they captured. Why? Primarily so that no black man could ever be a sexual threat to Muslim women in North African households. Secondly, Muslim slave owners themselves wanted to be the only ones to have sex with captive black women and girls, as Mohammed made lawful for them to do (see Koran 23:5 and 70:30). Muslim slave owners did not want black men competing with them as cohabiters with black women, so black men had to be emasculated.

Muslim slavers saw no need to breed slaves from slaves. Supplies were plentiful, prices reasonable. Thus, adding cynicism to depravity, Muslim slavers denied male African slaves not only freedom and wages, but even worse, the sacred human privileges of marriage, sex and parenting.

Evidence exists that Muslim slave owners did indeed step in to do what emasculated black males could not. Tens of millions of brown-skinned Haratin—people descended from the offspring of Arab fathers and black mothers—are found all across North Africa and, under different designations, in the Middle East. Mauritania alone is reported to have some 1 million Haratin.

In the United States, southern insistence on perpetuating slavery and northern opposition to it contributed to a bloody civil war in which 600,000 men died and 2 million others were wounded. The 10-year-long war in South Vietnam took 58,000 American lives, yet just one three-day battle at Gettysburg killed at least 51,000![8]

In which Muslim nation has there ever been even a minor civil disturbance of conscience—let alone a war—over slavery defined as evil? Not one! Yet Farrakhan, unwilling to give the northern states an ounce of credit for such a costly stand, praises Islam—still history's most heinous proslavery force—as a defender of the black race. Mother of all ironies!

Notes

1. Louis Farrakhan, interview by Larry King, *Larry King Live*, CNN, July 3, 1997.

2. Libyan leader Mu'ammar al-Qadhdhafi has promised Farrakhan at least $1 billion. Daniel Pipes, "The New Anti-Semitism," *Daniel Pipes.org*, October 16, 1997, http://www.danielpipes.org/article/288 (accessed September 24, 2002).

3. Louis Farrakhan, "Minister Farrakhan Challenges Black Men: Transcript from Minister Louis Farrakhan's Remarks at the Million Man March," *CNN*, October 17, 1995, http://www3.cnn.com/US/9510/megamarch/10-16/transcript/index.html (accessed October 28, 2002).

4. *Merriam-Webster's Collegiate Dictionary*, 10th ed., s.v. "slave," fr. *Sclavus* Slav; from the frequent enslavement of Slavs in central Europe.

5. Paul E. Pierson, source unknown.

6. "The Flourishing Business of Slavery," *The Economist*, September 21, 1996, n.p.

7. Daniel Pipes, *Militant Islam Reaches America* (New York: W. W. Norton and Company, 2002), p. 224.

8. "Kerry Angers Vietnamese Americans," *Daily Hampshire Gazette*, http://www.gazettenet.com/08192002/news/644489.htm (accessed October 28, 2002); "The Turning Point of the Civil War," *Gettysburg Pennsylvania Welcome Center*, http://www.gettysbg.com/battle.html (accessed October 28, 2002).

CHAPTER SIXTEEN

REVIEWING
MILITANT
ISLAM
REACHES
AMERICA

Dr. Daniel Pipes has written an epochal warning for America. Quotes from it may one day be inscribed in stone in a commemorative hall in Washington, D.C. Its title is *Militant Islam Reaches America.*[1]

Dr. Pipes was formerly an instructor at the University of Chicago and Harvard University. He has also served with the U.S. State Department and the Department of Defense. The author of 10 prior books, he is now director of the Philadelphia-based Middle East Forum. He is also a columnist for both the *New York Post* and the *Jerusalem Post.*

First let me explain what Dr. Pipes does not attempt in his book. He does not critique the Koran, as I do. In all his 309 pages, I found only three phrase-length quotes from the Koran. Nor does he closely examine Mohammed's deeds and the evident motives behind them—with one exception. Dr. Pipes describes a dubious stratagem related to the breaking in A.D. 630 of a pact Mohammed had ratified 22 months earlier with the people of Mecca—the Treaty of Hudaybiya.

Dr. Pipes does not seem to see the importance of the Western world confronting radical Islam by publicly exposing Mohammed as a self-discredited prophet and the Koran as a self-discrediting book. What a shame if radical Islam's Achilles' heel—Mohammed and the Koran's weird self-discreditation—should be wasted as a means of self-defense by the world they threaten.

Nor does Dr. Pipes anywhere mention the tens of thousands of radical Muslim madrasas that are providing militant Muslim leaders with a wealth of manpower resources that moderate Muslims do not have and are not even interested in seeking.

Dr. Pipes seems not to have read Bat Ye'or. He praises the accomplishments of Islamic civilization in past centuries as if it was all one unified, well-governed Eden.[2] He seems unaware of the violence, the kidnappings, the huge slave industry and the dire oppression through extortionary taxation of captive Jews and Christians during those hellish eras. He imagines that Islam became violently radicalized only in this century.

Dr. Pipes observes, "A militant Islamic state is almost by

definition a rogue state, not playing by any rules except those of expediency and power, a ruthless institution that causes misery at home and abroad. Islamists in charge means that conflicts proliferate, society is militarized, arsenals grow, and terrorism becomes an instrument of state. . . . Islamists repress moderate Muslims and treat non-Muslims as inferior specimens."[3]

Clearly Dr. Pipes does not realize that what he thinks describes only a *modern* Islamist state precisely describes innumerable Muslim caliphates and sultanates down through the centuries! When Dr. Pipes writes of "winning the war for the soul of Islam,"[4] one must reply, "Please tell us, professor—exactly when and where did that 'soul of Islam' ever find political manifestation? We need to know so we can recognize and applaud it if it ever recurs."

If Dr. Pipes's "soul of Islam" means noble character in idealistic Muslim individuals, that is believable, but that is not a political accomplishment one can try to duplicate. The sad truth is that there has never been even one enduring Muslim government that can be cited as a role model for a benign "soul of Islam" kind of state—certainly not under Mohammed, nor under the caliphs, the sultans or any government of the 55 Muslim nations existing today.

Alas, the good professor's vision of an ethereal yet somehow recoverable soul of Islam is only a "pipes-dream."

Yet in spite of the above omissions, Dr. Pipes strikes a thunderously loud gong. He documents the Islamic threat looming over America with startling quotes and lucid comments that swirl like snowflakes in a storm. In chapter 10, I cited Ibn Warraq's quotes from Kalim Siddiqui, director of London's Muslim Institute. Here are some of Dr. Pipes's comments about the teachings of an *American* Muslim activist with a like-sounding but differently spelled surname—Shamim A. Siddiqi:

Siddiqi [in writings Pipes finds available on Islamic web-
sites] argues that Muslims taking control of the United
States has more importance than such goals as sustain-
ing the Iranian revolution or destroying Israel, for it has
greater impact upon the future of Islam.[5]

Other Siddiqi opinions paraphrased by Pipes are:

To permit Islam to attain its rightful place requires that
"the ideology of Islam prevail over the mental horizon of
the American people." . . .

Establishing militant Islam in America would signal
the triumph of [militant Islam] . . . over its only rival, the
bundle of Christianity and liberalism that constitutes
Western civilization.[6]

Note that Siddiqi does not take Hinduism, Buddhism,
Taoism, etc., as seriously as Christianity and Western liberalism
when it comes to naming rivals Islam must overcome:

American Muslims . . . have the paramount responsibility of bringing Islam to power in their country.[7]

Siddiqi sees Islamists in power in Washington before
2020.[8]

Dr. Pipes names three primary means Islamists in America
are counting on to achieve their dream of an Islamicized
America: "immigration, reproduction and conversion."[9]

When Supreme Court Justice Harry Blackmun, his fellow
jurists and their counterparts in other Western nations began
making *Roe v. Wade*-like decisions in the 1960s and 1970s,
certainly they did not see themselves as favoring a rapid

depopulation of Western nations. Surely if they tried at all to foresee any consequences of such a radical decision, they would have assured themselves that no more than a small percentage of women would ever need or desire abortion on demand. No doubt they believed that a natural feminine instinct to love babies and prefer mothering to childlessness would prevail among a sufficiently large majority of Western women, guaranteeing continued Western population growth.

The justices were so direly wrong! While millions of women still choose marriage and childbearing, tens of millions have chosen catastrophically to abort one, two, three, four or more pregnancies! Caucasian-majority nations from Finland and Russia to the United States and Australia have thus plunged precipitously into population declines unmatched since the days of Europe's Black Plague. Add further declines due to media popularization of homosexuality—whose adherents are not noted for a strong interest in reproduction—and we find that dozens of Western nations are auto-genociding. Coffins outsell cradles.

To compensate for diminishing numbers of natives, Western nations must accept hundreds of millions of immigrants from the Middle East and other third-world regions. A large percentage of the immigrants flooding into the West are Muslims whose birthrates are substantially higher. Supremacist Islamic planners thus know that they have only to wait a few decades and the entire West will yield its present non-Muslim majorities to Islam. Justice Blackmun and company could hardly have aided supremacist Islam more handily if they had detonated weapons of mass destruction in 100 Western cities. An Islamic takeover of the world could be thus assured.

This is how reproduction—coupled with a lack of the same among Westerners—is a supremacist Islamic weapon probably far more dangerous than anything Saddam Hussein and others might concoct under the desert sands of the Middle East. *Roe v. Wade* and associated feminist philosophies absolutely must be revised if not reversed. The existence of a presumed female instinct to favor mothering is obviously less instinctive than was presumed. It is now very clear that culture has more to do with inspiring motherhood than messages encoded in DNA. The West must experience a massive return to ealier cultural norms or face extinction.[10]

Dr. Pipes quotes Siraj Wahhaj, an influential black convert to Islam, as saying to a Muslim audience in New Jersey late in 1992:

> "If we were united and strong, we'd elect our own emir [leader] and give allegiance to him. . . . Take my word, if 6-8 million Muslims unite in America, the country will come to us." If Muslims were more clever politically, Wahhaj told his listeners, they could take over the United States and replace the constitutional government with a caliphate.[11]

This from the first Muslim ever invited to offer an invocational prayer in the U.S. House of Representatives! Dozens of similar alarming quotes from American Muslims resound throughout Dr. Pipes's chapters.

Introducing a chapter called "The U.S. Government: Patron of Islam?" Dr. Pipes writes, "It was one thing to hear individual [pro-Islamic] statements by high government officials stretching back a decade and another thing to collect them, sort them, and ponder them. This latter task suggested a more cohesive and powerful message than had been evident from occasional remarks."[12]

Dr. Pipes adds that he and Mimi Stillman, coauthor of the chapter, wrote:

"By dismissing any connection between Islam and terrorism, complaining about media distortions, and claiming that America needs Islam," we concluded, official spokesmen "have turned the U.S. government into a discreet missionary for the [Islamic] faith." Assuming that is not their intention, the message of [the chapter mentioned] is that government officials should be much more careful when they speak about Islam.[13]

Dr. Pipes comments elsewhere,

It was not so long ago that Westerners could converse freely about Mohammed, Islam, Muslims and militant Islam, just as they still can about parallel Christian subjects. No longer. . . . Violence and intimidation have shut down the frank discussion of [Islam]. It has reached the strange point that, in a secular, Christian-majority country like the United States, a biographer of Jesus has freedom to engage in outrageous blasphemies while his counterpart working on Mohammed feels constrained to accept the pious Muslim version of the Prophet's life. I present this silencing as . . . a potential first step toward the imposition of Islamic law [in America].[14]

Then comes Dr. Pipes's sadly misplaced confidence that moderate Muslims are the knights who must somehow wage ideological warfare with radical Muslims for Dr. Pipes's mythical "soul of Islam." He admits, "Although the moderates appear—and in fact are—weak, they have a crucial role to play, for they alone can reconcile Islam with modernity."[15]

Elsewhere Dr. Pipes concedes, "The Internet has hundreds of militant Islamic sites but few traditionally pious ones."[16] Sites operated by *moderate* Muslims, as distinct from militant or traditional ones, are not even mentioned! Do any exist?

At the end of his tome, Dr. Pipes recommends that Western democracies should pin their hopes on helping Turkey—most democratic of all Muslim governments—launch a propaganda blitz to offer itself as a model for the establishment of democratic governments everywhere in the Islamic world. He acknowledges that Turkey is far from asking to step into the role and may even refuse.

We must learn to use quotes from Mohammed's Koran to undermine Muslim confidence in him and his writings.

But even if Turkey accepted, even if radical Muslims everywhere dropped their militant agendas and accepted Dr. Pipes's major American-led proposal, the Koran would still be there to generate anti-infidel hostility in another generation. Mohammed's example of treacherous atrocity would eventually inspire future Osama bin Ladens to arise.

We have no alternative. We must accept the solution that Mohammed himself unwittingly dropped in our very laps—use his own words, his own historical record to show that he discredited himself. We must learn to use quotes from his Koran to undermine Muslim confidence in him and his writings. Show them that turning away from Mohammed frees them to turn to God in truth. This calls for concerted efforts in winsome debate by millions of non-Muslims internationally. We in our millions must help millions of Muslims to see that what Islam loathes as the house of war is simply the human family of which they are an integral part!

Mohammed estranged them from us. Let us undo the estrangement. Win Muslims back into the human family under God!

Notes

1. Daniel Pipes, *Militant Islam Reaches America* (New York: W.W. Norton and Company, 2002).
2. Ibid., pp. 4, 74.
3. Ibid., p. 13.
4. Ibid., n.p.
5. Ibid., p. 114.
6. Ibid., p. 114.
7. Ibid., p. 115.
8. Ibid., p. 122.
9. Ibid., p. 118.
10. Patrick J. Buchanan, *The Death of the West* (New York: Thomas Dunne Books, 2002) pp. 1-49.
11. Pipes, *Militant Islam*, p. 112.
12. Ibid., p. xv.
13. Ibid., pp. xv-xvi.
14. Ibid., pp. xvii-xviii.
15. Ibid., p. xix.
16. Ibid., p. 15.

CHAPTER SEVENTEEN

WHAT SHOULD WE DO?

We live in a day when *every* president, *every* congressman, *every* prime minister, *every* governor, even every mayor, college president, school principal, editor, media interviewer, pastor and rabbi in the Western world must have objective knowledge of Mohammed, the Koran, the hadiths and Islam's supremacist goals. Readers may object: When we were threatened by fascism and later by communism, no one said allied leaders must peruse Hitler's *Mein Kampf* or Karl Marx's *Das Kapital*. Why should our leaders today care what is in the Koran and the hadiths?

Mein Kampf and *Das Kapital* were never virtually deified by 1.3 billion people.

Nor did Axis powers or communism ever achieve the microinfiltration that politicized Islam has already achieved through massive immigration into all Western nations. Dispersed among millions of Muslims who are peaceful, nonideologized immigrants are a few million others who are fanatically loyal to Mohammed's goal of total Islamic supremacy. These Muslims are more than religious. They are *politico*-religious.

BAD NEWS ABOUT MISINFORMATION

Suicide bombers among Muslim radicals—unless armed with weapons of mass destruction—paradoxically are less dangerous. Suicide bombers blow up themselves and a limited number of others and are gone, or they blow their cover instead and are arrested before they cause harm. Suicide bombers tend to be either brainwashed youths or not-very-bright adults. The more dangerous radical Muslims are the brainwashers. They may be mullahs teaching in mosques or madrasas, heads of Islamic charitable organizations, writers in Islamic newsletters, embassy personnel or professors subverting our sons and daughters with Islamic propaganda on Western campuses.

They are the *intelligent* Muslims.

Westerners in positions of leadership, if uninformed, will be impressed and naively taken in by them again and again. The result: laws will be passed, legal precedents set and school courses introduced that are biased in favor of Islam. One-sided laws, legal precedents and education, over the long-term, may do more *crucial* damage than exploding bombs.

Islam did not build our Western civilization. If the many institutions that did contribute to building our society merit no special favors, why should Islam?

My website, featured later in this book, offers books about Islam—some of which are quoted in this volume. Careful readers of this book and other books will be able then to intrigue their friends by asking them questions they can't answer—making them aware of how much they in turn need to learn.

This book is but a 256-page study. I strongly recommend, in spite of anti-Judeo-Christian passages that make me hold my nose, Ibn Warraq's 400-page tome. He garners facts from Muir, Rodinson, Bat Ye'or and hundreds of Muslim sources. I also value David Pryce-Jones's *The Closed Circle*.[1] (See full bibliography at the back of this book.)

Naiveté Right to the Top

President Bush is a good president and a very likeable man. But he is, like seemingly every other Western head of state, uneducated about Islam. The fact that he, shortly after 9/11, would publicly call America's war on terror "a crusade" revealed his naiveté.[2] The fact that none of his advisors warned him against

> For many liberal-minded Americans, the mere fact that 1.3 billion Muslims believe in the Koran makes the message in the book as good as true.

that word until after he used it reveals their naiveté, too. Hence my first recommendation: We must all try to prompt our leaders in every category of society, in effect, to go back to school and seek objectivity regarding Islam.

President Bush should take the lead by stating publicly that Islam is, after all, a religion with supremacist practical goals, and that he as our leader is now devoting time to learn why that is so.

Instead, President Bush openly refers to Islam as a great religion and a religion of peace. I understand his predicament. He must not speak words that might incite some Americans to vigilantism. At the same time, he should try to avoid positivistic overstatement. We *do* have a problem—how do we defend against the supremacist Muslim wolf at our door without waking the dog of vigilantism?

For many liberal-minded Americans, the mere fact that 1.3 billion Muslims believe in the Koran makes the message in the book as good as true. They think we must call it good out of respect for the sheer masses of people whose minds are umbilically linked to it.

As tons of rock press rotting vegetation until it becomes coal, oil or even a valuable diamond, similarly the faith of 1.3 billion Muslims in effect supposedly transforms Mohammed's venom into something socially useful, like olive oil. Actually, as the number of people who hear the Muslim God speaking through every war verse in the Koran grows, so grows the Koran as a threat. Mohammed's venom remains venom, but ordinary people sufficiently poisoned by it can become crafty fanatics, if not crazed terrorists.

The Oath to Uphold the Constitution

Beyond this there is another aspect to our problem: Every immigrant seeking to be naturalized as an American citizen must swear to uphold the U.S. Constitution. New Testament-guided Christians, along with Jews, have no problem taking that oath. Muslims who swear that oath but also believe that *God* speaks through every war verse in the Koran are very seriously perjuring themselves!

The Constitution prevents religion from controlling the state. The Koran, via Sharia law and the Sunna (a collection of rules for Muslims to obey), *demands* Islamic control over all civil authority. It also claims the right to replace any and every nation's laws with Sharia law. Laws consistent with our Constitution forbid murder, slavery and prostitution—all of which are endorsed by the Koran. Our Constitution guarantees equal rights before the law for both sexes. The Koran equates one man's testimony with that of *two* women (see Koran 2:282).

If the oath that grants an immigrant citizenship in this great nation is to be meaningful, not a farce, the Immigration and Naturalization Service (INS) must confront the fact that perhaps as many as several million Muslims committed de facto perjury to become naturalized. Millions more who regard themselves as devoted to the Koran will also readily perjure themselves to become naturalized—if a legal line is not drawn.

Indeed, some Muslims may be unaware that Islam is radically opposed to something as major as the separation of the state from religious control. No matter, the INS must be required by an act of Congress to make every Muslim aware of this innate contradiction between the Koran and the U.S. Constitution and to require every Muslim applicant for naturalization to declare under oath that he or she sides with the Constitution, not the Koran, in so major a matter.

Our tragically uninformed government got us into this situation by appointing equally uninformed INS officials who unjustifiably assume that one religion is essentially like any other. The argument in their minds must go something like this: Christians and Jews genuinely accept our Constitution and blend in, so *of course*, Muslims will, too. No doubt many do, but some already-naturalized Muslims harbor other ideas. Mohammed taught that a Muslim's commitment to Islam supercedes every other bond. Thus the fact that a Muslim may be a fellow citizen does not guarantee that he holds our national interests higher than Islam's international goals.

Policymakers who for the most part cannot imagine themselves being earnest about matters of faith have trouble believing how utterly serious about religion certain other people can be. What little knowledge our policymakers have about Islam is usually heavily mythologized and pathetically trivial.

The Five Pillars

Some Americans in leading roles think they are sufficiently educated about Islam if, for example, they can name the so-called five pillars of Islam (faith, prayer, purification, fast and pilgrimage). But if they do not know that radical Islam has only *one* genuine pillar—*jihad*—and that it has worldwide political dominion as its goal, they remain essentially uninformed. The so-called five pillars of Islam, by comparison with radical Islam's jihad, are merely five little candles flickering atop Islam's primary pillar—the political one. The five little candles add a nicely distracting religious décor, but little more.

Quizzing by the INS

How can the INS protect the integrity of the naturalization oath when a Muslim applies for citizenship? A cue can be taken from already existing INS procedure.

The INS knows, for example, that some people are conscientious objectors, such as Christians who believe the New Testament forbids them to take up arms even for personal self-preservation, let alone national defense. Accordingly, when I applied for U.S. citizenship, my interviewer queried, "If asked by the government, are you willing to bear arms for the defense of the United States of America?" With Romans 13:1-4 in mind, I unhesitatingly and sincerely said, "Yes."

What would have happened had I said, "No"? Would my application have been rejected? I have no inkling. The point I make is this: If *that* query can be asked by the INS without objection, surely other similar questions that probe the influence of an individual's personal beliefs upon his relationship with the Constitution could be asked also.

There could be one set of questions fitted, like the already existing one above, for those who declare Christianity as their religion, another for those who declare Judaism and, of course, one for those who follow Islam. A fitting question for Muslims could be, "Do you believe the United States of America would ultimately benefit by submitting to Islam's Sharia law?" A yes answer violates the constitutional requirement separating the state from religious control.

Questioning Hindus, Too

To be fair, Hindus should also be queried. Some Hindus in India are actually pressuring the government there to reinstate an ancient requirement of Hinduism called suttee—a belief that a Hindu widow must be burned alive on or beside the pyre on which her husband's body is cremated. It matters not if she is a mother with dependent children or decades younger than her husband. If she outlives her spouse, she disgraces him, herself and his and her families both.

Suttee was abolished under British colonial control around the end of the eighteenth century. As soon as India became independent in 1947, some Hindus, not all, began clamoring for suttee to be reinstated. Thus far the government of India has resisted their pressure.

Surely any Hindu who would want his widow or any other woman to be burned alive should not be granted a transfer of citizenship to *any* nation. Let him remain in the land of his birth and be that land's problem.

Responding to Bad Opinions

When religion-based *opinions*, even apart from actual *deeds* resulting from them, contradict Western law, there exists a valid basis for denying visas and citizenship to people seeking access to or citizenship in free Western nations.

Granted, no one can be put on trial for holding a bad opinion. A bad opinion must first result in a bad deed. But denying a visa, green card or citizenship is *not* putting someone on trial. In such matters, we have a right to select people according to their opinions, just as lawyers do when selecting jurors from a jury pool.

To choose otherwise is to elevate cultural pluralism above the rule of law. Thus I recommend that concerned citizens urge the INS to provide officials with questions to test applicants for visas, green cards or citizenship—as if they are lawyers selecting jurors from a jury pool.

WHEN WE SHARE THE AIRWAVES

On another topic: Christians invited to represent Christianity opposite Muslims in media interviews must learn to represent us effectively. This is especially true in the presence of secular interviewers, some of whom tend to side with Muslim interviewees, mistakenly viewing them as underdogs who probably cannot manage without some help.

When either a Muslim or a Muslim-sympathizing host thrusts with "You are against Islam!" a responder may parry with "Now that I know that a major part of Islam has dictatorial goals, yes, as a free man, I oppose supremacist Islam as honorably as my parents opposed fascism and communism in their generation."

Have ready a quote from Siddiqi or Badawi (see chapter 9). David Price-Jones's *The Closed Circle* also has excellent quotables.

If a Muslim counters with "Islam is not opposed to democracy," ask, "Why then is there not a single true democracy in the entire Muslim world?" Cite the *Newsweek* article showing that even the most liberal of 55 Muslim nations, Turkey, is still far from ideal in guaranteeing individual human rights.

When either a Muslim or a host hurls the predictable "You are a Muslim basher!" reply, "Islam is its own Muslim basher because it denies basic freedoms to its own people, especially Muslim women. I could not possibly want to bash 1.3 billion people who merit so much sympathy for the loss of their freedoms."

Or you could say, "A Muslim basher is someone with a personal vendetta against Muslims. You misspeak when you apply so ugly a label to someone who is merely criticizing Islam as a system of thought."

When facing—in front of a secular audience—the question, "Do you as a Christian believe that God does not hear the prayers of Jews or Muslims?" I recommend, "God is not deaf. He hears every prayer in the universe 10 million years before it is prayed. How He may answer or decline to answer any given person's prayer is too deep a theological question for this brief interview."

The preceding question will likely be followed by, "Do you believe Muslims are going to hell?" The very question is, of course, hostile bait on a hook. The asker realizes that any Christian who says "Yes" will appear bigoted before a general audience. If he says "No," he will sound like a wimpy compromiser in the eyes of conservative Christians. But there *is* a way to reply: "A more germaine question is, 'Does the Koran itself warn that *we* as infidels and even many Muslims are going to hell?' Yes! In 783 verses! Not only infidels like us but also Muslims who refuse to war against us will burn in hell forever. So—if the Koran is to be believed, yes, many Muslims will be in hell.

"Several hadiths count far more Muslim women already burning in hell than Muslim men. Why? Hadithic logic reasons it is because they were so ungrateful for their husbands' kindnesses.

"With specious threats like that hanging over their heads, we have still another reason why Muslim women especially merit sympathy from the entire world."

A longer answer, though invariably much more satisfying for Christian listeners, is almost always interrupted, hence self-defeating. But if a longer answer is indeed possible, one may add, "The Bible also warns of hell, but proclaims Jesus as mankind's sinless mediating redeemer—God incarnate who atoned for the sin of the world at Calvary. Jesus is the One who saves from judgment every one who confesses his or her sinfulness and asks forgiveness through Him.

Islam has no redeemer, no mediator and no forgiveness guarantor.

"Islam, conversely, has no redeemer, no mediator and no forgiveness guarantor. Under Islam, every human defendant in God's court must face the ultimate judge without the help of an advocate. Hence, under Islam, there can be no assurance regarding one's eternal destiny."

According to the Koran, any individual's prognosis is gloomy at best. Even Mohammed doubted his chance of entering paradise. In a volume of hadiths called *An-Nawawi's Forty Hadiths*, Mohammed is quoted as saying:

Verily one of you behaves like the people of Paradise until there is but an arm's length between him and it [paradise]. [Then] that which was written [long ago, as God's predetermining will] overtakes him, and so he behaves like the people of Hell-fire and thus he enters it [hell]. And one of you behaves like the people of Hell-fire until there is but an arm's length between him and it [hell]. Then that which was written overtakes him and so he behaves like the people of Paradise and thus he enters it.[3]

Not content merely to shake any Muslim's confidence of gaining access to paradise, Mohammed took a further step that destroys a Muslim's assurance that he will even be allowed to remain in paradise once admitted! In verse 11:107, Mohammed dictated:

As for the blessed, they shall abide in paradise as long as the heavens and the earth endure, *unless your Lord ordain otherwise*. Theirs shall be an endless recompense (Koran, emphasis added**).**

Clearly any Muslim must face the possibility that his "endless recompense" may begin in paradise but end up in the only other eternal abode the Koran mentions—*hell!*

Jesus presented God the father to mankind as a deity who is immediately and eternally faithful. God as presented by Mohammed is worse than fickle or arbitrary—he could be diagnosed as schizophrenic!

Since even an honest, moral Muslim cannot know until the final seconds which fate God predetermined for him or her ages ago, he or she faces an unnerving prospect indeed. God's whimsical predetermination can incite a good person to a few final seconds of evil, thus nullifying a lifelong pursuit of goodness.

But the issue of who goes or does not go to hell needs a more detailed treatment, which I provide in appendix A.

THE NAMES OF ALLAH
AND OTHERS

Considering what we have learned of Mohammed's concept of Allah here and in earlier chapters, does the name Allah qualify for acceptance as a valid alias for God? Koranic and hadithic passages like the ones in this chapter lead many Christians and perhaps Jews as well to protest that the Muslim's God is some pseudodeity other than the Judeo-Christian God. On this basis some people urge Judeo-Christians to reject all use of Allah as an alternate name for the God of the Bible. Yet Muslims affirm him as the uncreated creator of the heavens and Earth.

Arguments that Mohammed derived the very name Allah from the name of a pagan deity Ilah seem ill-founded. Residents of Mecca, instead of running Mohammed out of town, would simply have laughed him out of town had he tried to accomplish that huge a switch in the meaning of a well-known name.

A more likely scenario notes the resemblance between the linguistic cognates "Allah" and "Eloh"; i.e., the Hebrew name Elohim, minus the plural suffix "im." If this is indeed the real origin of Allah, then Allah is valid as an alias—an AKA—for Elohim. But what about Mohammed's deliberate infusion of bad character into the name Allah?

Suppose that we know that a man named John Smith is an honest, moral, just person. If some other people besmirch John Smith's good name, dragging it in the mud, should John Smith change his name? If he does, the besmirchers will vilify that name, too. Surely John Smith is better advised to continue to be known as John Smith and let ignorant men be responsible for their own abuse of his worthy name. Of course, friends of John Smith, when they use his name, will carefully qualify for the ignorant what they do and do not mean when using his name.

Still More on Islamic Revisionism

God is not the only one whose character Mohammed's redefinitions still defame through the Koran and the hadiths, 1,400 years later.

Acknowledging Jesus as virgin born, sinless and a worker of miracles, Mohammed still omitted the most crucial thing—the Lord's death and resurrection, as I have previously noted. Various hadiths show Mohammed curiously affirming something else from the New Testament but, once again, with ghastly revisions.

It is Jesus' second coming.

Hadiths agree that Jesus is coming back to judge mankind, but what an unbiblical judgment it will be! Jesus, Mohammed declared, will destroy the Cross, meaning Christianity. He will

Mohammed's utter contempt for Christians and Jews carries forward in Islam today.

command all Christians and all Jews to convert to Islam and command Muslims everywhere to exterminate every Christian and every Jew who refuses conversion.

Christians and Jews who refuse to convert will flee and hide behind rocks and trees, but in vain. Allah will cause rocks and trees to sprout mouths, shouting to the Muslims, "There's a Christian (or a Jew) hiding behind me. Come, Muslim, come and kill him!"

Mohammed's utter contempt for Christians and Jews carries forward in Islam today. When I visited Saudi Arabia years ago, I learned that the Saudi government once objected to a Swissair jet landing in the kingdom because it had a cross painted on its tail. I was told that mutawas, the Saudi religious police, tear necklaces with crosses from the necks of foreign visitors in the streets. Banners and ads offer financial rewards to Saudis who inform on fellow Saudis who attend a Christian meeting or harbor a Bible. Foreign workers who convert to Islam are given a financial reward. Saudis who convert to Christianity are beaten, imprisoned and occasionally beheaded.

Let the whole world be warned that the toleration Islam demands when it is a minority is not reciprocated when it takes control.

Notes

1. David Pryce-Jones, *The Closed Circle: An Interpretation of the Arabs* (New York: HarperCollins, 1991), n.p.
2. Sally Buzbee, "Bush's Use of the Word 'Crusade' a Red Flag," *Seattle Post-Intelligencer*, September 18, 2001. http://seattlepi.nwsource.com/national/39266_crusade18.shtml (accessed October 28, 2002).
3. Imam An-Nawawi, "An-Nawawi's Forty Hadiths (number 4)," *International Islamic University Malaysia*. http://www.iiu.edu.my/deed/hadith/other/hadithnawawi.html (accessed October 28, 2002).

X-RAYING THE SECRETS

Every major religion is based upon a body of foundational literature. Judaism has its Tenach, consisting of the Torah, Psalms and Prophets. Christianity has its New Testament, perceived by Christians as fulfilling Judaism's Tenach. Hinduism has its Vedas and Upanishads. Buddhism has the writings of Gautama. Islam has its Koran and hadiths. Surely it is also true that each major religion's ability to survive is linked to the ability of its founding literature to remain *relevant* as aeons pass.

If a religion teaches that the world rests on the back of an elephant who in turn stands upon the shells of four turtles, that religion *merits* a loss of credibility as scientific knowledge increases. Some biologists will claim that evolutionary theory just as assuredly invalidates the premise in other religious writings that God exists and engineered mankind as a special creation made in His image, but this is still debatable.

Likewise a religion that requires widows to be burned alive on the funeral pyres of their deceased husbands should *also* lose credibility as recognition of the intrinsic moral and intellectual equivalence of the sexes spreads.

The trouble is, a modern trend wants to vindicate every religion no matter what it teaches. Rules of reasonableness are laid aside. In law, good cops are good; rogue cops are bad. In medicine, good doctors are good; quacks are bad. But in religion, strangely, everything is somehow good; nothing is essentially bad. This is self-deceived nonsense, and we can no longer afford it.

History shows that the Old Testament and especially the New Testament carefully studied and followed inspire goodwill, charity and self-sacrifice. Christian tenets encourage the granting of human rights and the sharing of political power and responsibility. Most important, the Bible encourages reliance upon charisma, not violence, as the primary instrument for countering evil. Yet Christianity, disconnected from New Testament teachings, becomes pseudo-Christianity, and pseudo-Christianity can be very *bad*. The watching world has the right to X-ray Christianity and pseudo-Christianity on moral grounds and peg their respective pluses and minuses. But let every other religion also be X-rayed on the same basis of morality and reason and be rated accordingly.

It is my contention in this book that if the world would only decide to X-ray the Koran on moral grounds, its utter lack of integrity will be readily evident. In this book I have sought to show a major part of what that X ray will reveal. X rays have a way of dispelling naiveté. What was thought to be just an upset stomach turns out to be pancreatic cancer. Similarly, what is touted as a peace-inspiring book is shown, in reality, to be a guidebook for dictatorial world dominion at any cost.

Just as cancers are attacked with chemo and radiation therapy, the Western world must irradiate the Koran with a bombardment of logical debate that debunks its false claims. This treatment will of course trigger anger that heightens to rage and results even in violence in some areas. But if the irradiation persists and is sufficiently widespread, logic and sanity will eventually win the day. By the millions, Muslims will admit the truth and be set free. Then at least our children and grandchildren will not be as threatened by supremacist Islam as we are now.

CHRISTIANITY'S AGE-LONG EXCLUSIVIST/ INCLUSIVIST CONTROVERSY

Interviewers questioning Christian spokespersons ranging from members of the Billy Graham family to Pat Robertson to Jerry Falwell are wont to ask, "Do you believe all Muslims are going to hell?" Most of the replies given either affirm or imply a yes. The issue of who do Christians think goes to hell and who do they think doesn't has thus become a controversy connected with the events of September 11, 2001. Since the issue, from the Christian side, hinges upon New Testament Scripture, what does the New Testament *really* say on the question?

Most New Testament-honoring Christians hold to one of two views on the question of who will be saved and who will be lost. One view is called *exclusivism*, the other *inclusivism*. Both views credit Christ's atoning sacrifice as the only basis whereby the infinitely holy creator of the universe can forgive sin without compromising Himself by not punishing it. (Does not a judge dishonor the law, government, people and himself if he fails to *enforce* the law?)

A lawbreaker's ignorance of the law and/or his regret for misdeeds and/or his subsequent doing of good deeds may give a judge basis to moderate a penalty, but not to acquit! Enforcement is enforcement. To expect God to overlook sin at the cost of breaching His own holy nature just adds another sin! Only if the judge himself voluntarily pays the fine, endures the pain and takes the loss is forgiveness possible. *That* is what the New Testament shows Jesus, our judge, doing for us, thus becoming our Savior! The New Testament uniquely proclaims a divine provision of atonement for mankind's sin through the self-sacrifice of Jesus the Messiah.

The New Testament also proclaims uniquely that Jesus' self-sacrifice happened in explicit fulfillment of Old Testament prophecy, making His self-sacrifice *Judeo*-Christian, not just Christian. There is hardly anything more central to Judeo-Christianity than *divine atonement*, yet that is a concept Mohammed loathed and denied, rendering Islam antithetical in the extreme to Judeo-Christianity.

Still, a further question remains to be resolved by a study of the New Testament: What does an individual have to do to receive forgiveness through the atonement that Jesus, the judge who is also the Savior, provides? That is the question that divides exclusivist Christians from their inclusivist brothers and sisters.

LOOKING AT POINTS OF AGREEMENT

To put it in New Testament words, both groups agree with John 14:6. That is where Jesus declared, *"I am the way and the truth and the life. No one comes to the Father except through me."* How else do both camps agree? Most advocates of both views agree that all who die as babies or as little children enjoy automatic redemption coverage through the atoning self-sacrifice of Jesus (see Romans 7:9). But both groups tend to be unaware of a significant estimate medical historians have made regarding the world's *average* infant mortality rates down through history.

 If a majority of people created in God's likeness are lost, God has lost an enormous part of a precious commodity—His likeness!

I will always remember a report I read two decades ago. A group of scientists estimated that some 66 percent of everyone conceived in the womb has not survived to see even a fifth year of life. This means that two-thirds of mankind have died either in the womb through miscarriage, stillbirth or abortion, *or* in childhood via disease, crime, war, accidents or natural disasters. Thus a large majority of all the people God has created in His likeness from the beginning of humankind are redeemed by this automatic childhood coverage aspect of redemption.

Consider this: If a majority of people created in God's likeness are lost, God has lost an enormous part of a very precious commodity—His likeness! In that event God will have won only the moral victory over evil. Evil will have won the quantitative victory over God by causing far more people to be lost than are redeemed. In fact, redemption's automatic childhood coverage clause guarantees that far more people are redeemed than are lost (see Isaiah 57:1).

Take medical science's 66 percent estimate on infant mortality through the ages as a mere base number. Add hundreds of millions who, through the ages, lost their redemption by sinning as they came out of childhood but found it again by responding to revelation from God. Estimates of the combined total point to perhaps 77 percent of mankind redeemed! God wins not only the moral victory but the quantitative one as well!!

A further point of agreement pertains to a time limit for repentance on the part of the lost! Repentance must occur before death, not after. The New Testament warns, *"Man is destined to die once, and after that to face judgment . . . for the things done while in the body, whether good or bad"* (Hebrews 9:27; 2 Corinthians 5:10).

DEFINING THE ISSUES AND DIFFERENCES

However, from this point on the exclusivist/inclusivist disagreement begins to rankle. Here's why: The Bible affirms not one but two categories of revelation that God has given to mankind. Exclusivists believe that Jesus employs only one of the two categories of revelation to reredeem people who lost redemption coming out of childhood. They are called exclusivists because they *exclude* the possibility that Jesus may also employ the other category of revelation to draw people lost since emerging from childhood innocence through repentance to faith, and thereby to redemption restored.

Inclusivists, by contrast, are so named because they *include* either or both categories of revelation as instruments Jesus uses to draw lost people to repentance and faith, and thereby to redemption restored.

The Role of Revelation

What *are* the two categories of revelation?

One is called *general revelation*—the witness of the heavens and the earth, described, for example, in Psalm 19:1-4 and Romans 1:19-20. Creation itself imparts to us general knowledge about God as creator and sustainer, hence the name general revelation. It is called general for a second reason as well: Everyone who lives in this world encounters it. In that sense also it is general.

Exclusivists see the knowledge general revelation imparts to all lost people as enabling them to feel guilty and condemned because of their sin, but nothing more. That knowledge by itself is not sufficient, exclusivists declare, to lead lost people beyond feeling guilty and condemned to actual repentance and faith, and therefore to redemption. Exclusivists thus *exclude* general revelation as a bringer of salvation in the hands of the Jesus of John 14:6.

Exclusivists believe that Jesus—in addition to the coverage He supplies for children—applies the saving benefit of His atoning death to redeem only those people who, learning the historically revealed name "Jesus" through the other kind of revelation—New Testament special revelation—pray specifically to Him by that name, asking to be redeemed by His atoning death.

The Name of Jesus

This view derives mainly from Acts 4:12, *"There is* no other name *under heaven given to men by which we must be saved"* (emphasis added).

Inclusivists—so called because they *include* general revelation as one of Jesus' John 14:6 redemptive instruments—reply as follows: Peter, who spoke the words quoted in Acts 4:12, was a Hebrew, and Hebrews—from antiquity—frequently used the noun "name" idiomatically. It was simply Peter's Hebraic synonym for "person." Peter meant that the Person, Jesus, is mankind's only Savior. He would be quite surprised, inclusivists say, to find anyone thinking He meant that the *name* of Jesus and the *person* of Jesus are two distinct entities, *both* of which have to be involved before anyone's salvation is actuated.

Of course exclusivists carry their understanding of Acts 4:12 over to John 14:6 itself. Inclusivists reply that John 14:6 simply explains *what Jesus offers*, but does *not* explain what a supplicant needs to do to avail himself of it. Does a supplicant have to pray to Jesus *by name* in order to come to the Father through Him? Or, if he just prays in faith to the creator God of general revelation, does Jesus, incognito, just as readily bring him to the Father? Inclusivists say yes! Jesus incognito is just as much the Savior as Jesus named!

Exclusivists also find basis for their view in Romans 10:9, which reads, "*If you confess with your mouth, 'Jesus is Lord,' and believe in your heart that God raised him from the dead, you will be saved.*" Inclusivists believe that Romans 10:9 describes how people find salvation through Christ *when New Testament special revelation* has been proclaimed to them. In other words, it is the main way, the preferred way, that people access the redemption that is found only in Jesus. That people lacking knowledge of the New Testament can be redeemed just as surely by the incognito Jesus, inclusivists say, is borne out by Paul's quote from Joel 2:32—written before the name of Jesus was known—just four verses later in Romans 10:13: "*Everyone who calls on the name of the Lord will be saved*" (emphasis added).

If a supplicant for salvation does not have to call to the actual *name* of Jesus in the context of the Christian gospel, what *does* he need to respond to? The inclusivist answer is, *at least* the witness of God via all the wondrous aspects of the heavens and the earth, commonly called *general revelation.*

Do inclusivists believe that Jesus uses general revelation to redeem *everyone* that New Testament revelation—for whatever reason—does not bring in? Not at all! If inclusivists believed that, they would no longer be inclusivists, but rather *universalists*—i.e., extremely liberal people who somehow believe God can be God without punishing evil. In a universalist's view, even Hitler and Stalin will be welcomed into paradise. In other words, God has no problem breaching His holiness to save the wicked, or perhaps has no holiness to be breached!

Inclusivists believe that some people spurn the witness of creation—just as others spurn the witness of both creation and the gospel. Accordingly, they miss out on redemption and are lost forever.

Exclusivists aver that if inclusivist views prevail, Christian motivation to spread the gospel worldwide will be among the lost! Inclusivists reply that many who spurn the witness of creation in the absence of the gospel are drawn to repentance and faith when the gospel confirms the prior witness. Hence our human proclamation of the gospel is still an absolute necessity.

Even those already redeemed by Christ incognito via general revelation urgently need our human witness, inclusivists affirm, to have the basis of their salvation *elucidated* and to be equipped with the full counsel of God for more effective service in the Kingdom.

Thus inclusivists believe that Jesus does indeed save people anywhere who respond to all the wonders around them by asking the maker of it all to be merciful to them on whatever basis He may have to forgive the guilty. Inclusivists quote Hebrews 11:6: *"Anyone who comes to [God] must believe that he exists and that he rewards those who earnestly seek him."*

A plain formula indeed!

Inclusivists also point to Romans 2:7: *"To those who by persistence in doing good seek glory, honor and immortality, he* [God] *will give eternal life."* This verse makes no mention of praying to Jesus *by name.* Acts 17:26 and 27 agree essentially with the inclusivist understanding of the above two passages.

To counter this view, exclusivists further quote Romans 10:17: *"Faith comes from hearing the message, and the message is heard through the word of Christ."* Inclusivists respond that Paul, by quoting from Psalm 19:4's reference to the witness of creation in the very next verse, verse 18, conceives of general revelation in creation as part and parcel of that word of Christ through which faith arises, leading to salvation.

Exclusivists quote Acts 11:14 to show by the witness of an angel that even a pagan as noble as Cornelius, a Roman centurion, was not redeemed until Peter preached the name of Jesus to him. Inclusivists show that three earlier witnesses—quoted in Acts 10:4-6, 10:22 and 10:30-32—confirm that the angel did not actually say to Cornelius all that Peter later told the committee he said.

Abashed by the criticism of his peers in Jerusalem, Peter seems to have padded his narrative a little, hoping to cool the hot seat.

This view allows that Peter's preaching may have meant salvation for members of Cornelius's household, but for Cornelius himself, Peter's preaching brought *affirmation* and *elucidation* only—still a major contribution to Cornelius's spiritual well-being.

Considering God's Judgment

I know one inclusivist who draws upon the Old Testament's Psalm 50:1-6, in which a host of people summoned *"from the rising of the sun to the place where it sets"* are subjected to God's judgment. The witnesses that God calls to judge them fairly are not the Law and the prophets of biblical revelation to which they had no access. Instead, God *"summons the heavens above* [the heavens that in verse 6 *"proclaim His righteousness"*] *and the earth, that he may judge"* those assembled. Thus God judges them according to how they responded to general revelation's witness, because that was the only revelation they had.

The next question is, When God judges *that* category of people in *that* kind of a court, are any saved or are all condemned? Verse 5 assures us that some are acquitted. After the judging is done, God says, *"Gather to me my consecrated ones, who made a covenant with me by sacrifice."*

Many people were redeemed by believing in covenants *God* made through Old Testament patriarchs.

Many people were redeemed by believing in covenants *God* made through Old Testament patriarchs. Others find salvation through the *new, fully elucidating* covenant God made via Jesus the Messiah. But Psalm 50:5 speaks of people who, responding to the less elucidating testimony of general revelation, make their own individual covenants with God by sacrifice. Who then is their Savior? Inclusivists affirm—none other than the eternal *logos,* Jesus incognito.

Inclusivists may also point to John 3:21, which speaks of everyone who *"lives by the truth"* and does what they do *"through God"*—*before* he or she *"comes into the light"*! Clearly any truth people live by before they come to the light—the light of special revelation—must be by the light of general revelation.

Inclusivists follow John 3:21 with John 10:16—the passage where Jesus claims to have *"other sheep"* whom he intends to *"bring,"* making *two already existing sheep pens one!* Could that be a reference to his scattered general-revelation believers for whom he intends to provide elucidation through us? Inclusivists believe so.

Exclusivists acknowledge that people were redeemed apart from knowing the name of Jesus in Old Testament eras, but now that He has been revealed in the world, everyone has to pray to Jesus *by name* to be redeemed. Inclusivists reply, "That makes God like a referee in a football game who changes the rules at halftime, but tells only one team."

So when an exclusivist and a Muslim square off in public, each can describe the other as hell-bound. An audience that does not believe in God—or does not believe that God punishes evil— may feel inclined to mutter, "A pox on both your houses."

An inclusivist, however, can look a Muslim, Hindu or Buddhist in the eye and say, "If you are a redeemed person, it is because Jesus has redeemed you, though you do not know it is He. And your redemption is not to the credit of Mohammed or the Koran or Krishna or Gautama Buddha but to Jesus. God drew you at some point to true faith in Him via the witness of Old Testament revelation and/or the witness of His creation around you, whereupon Jesus redeemed you. But now He wants you to know—through the *elucidation* of the New Testament Gospels— *who* He really is and *how* He obtained redemption for you."

Conversely, if you are *not* already redeemed by Jesus incognito, Jesus *named* stands ready to redeem you here and now, pending your sincere supplication to Him.

Christian reader—decide which view *you* believe is biblically valid. Your decision will influence how you bear witness for Christ to non-Christians.

I warn, however, that the extreme hatred the Koran foments against the true Jesus of the New Testament—and against Christians and Jews—does not bode well for inclusivism's "Jesus incognito" redeeming radical Muslims. A hating heart does not easily respond to general—let alone special—revelation. And apart from a heartfelt response to God, the Bible promises *no salvation.*

If you are *not* already redeemed by Jesus incognito, Jesus *named* stands ready to redeem you here and now.

How Television Interviews Can Express *Nonverbal* Antagonism Toward an Interviewee

A television interviewer invited a Protestant minister to his program to comment on Islam. The minister chose to drive home one point: Mohammed married a six-year-old girl named Aisha and consummated the marriage with her when she was nine years old. *Ergo,* Mohammed was a pedophile.

The startled interviewer—lacking even a smidgeon of background on the topic, grinned defensively, trying to brush the statement off as a joke. Ill-advisedly, the minister was also grinning, undercutting the seriousness of his charge. Suddenly the camera, *always* maintaining a respectful distance from the host and the other guests, disrepectfully zoomed in so close to the minister that viewers could almost see into the very pores on his chin. That intrusively up-close shot made the minister's face appear huge and quivery, even foreshortened, which looks unnatural.

The minister's appearance, unflattering as almost anyone's would be at such close range, was deliberately distorted by a cameraman or perhaps by a program controller to distract viewers from what he was saying to the audience.

I have never known a television camera to come in that close on a Muslim interviewee. A close-up camera shot is a sure sign that someone in or behind a program *despises* whoever is unfortunate enough to be in front of the lens.

Clearly the interviewer and the cameraman were *not* eager to gain a single important insight about Islam from the minister. They *only* wanted to ridicule him and all conservative Christians with him. In the future, the minister should demand in writing that the camera, whenever turned toward him, must politely show him from the top of his head at least to the middle of his tie.

If a Muslim interviewee had been present, no doubt he would have countered that six-year-old Aisha's father voluntarily *gave* her to Mohammed to wed, so how dare the minister call Mohammed a pedophile? "Pedophile" describes someone who molests a child covertly.

Would the minister have had an answer? Hopefully he would have said, "A true 'prophet' would have the self-restraint to reject such an ill-advised offer from any parent!"

How Pervasive the Spirit of Compromise with Islam Can Be

Some secular authors—even Rodinson—after exposing Mohammed's murders, treachery, enslavement, beheadings, plundering and fraud, still end their books by compromising with the very evil they have so effectively exposed to the sunlight of public opinion. They compromise by commending Mohammed just because he managed ultimately to "influence" more than a billion people. Thus do these authors illogically accept a form of *might makes right* philosophy. In this instance, it is the might of large *numbers* that makes right. Perhaps they fear physical retaliation if the exposure of the wickedness of so fraudulent a prophet leaves radical Muslims very upset.

I am not so inclined. We must, in a manner that respects Muslims as people, confront them with the facts. Then let the facts themselves bear down heavily upon the conscience of Muslims. Ask them, How can they with good conscience take so despicable a murderer as their example? How can they recommend so consummate a liar as an example for us and as a spokesman for God?

Muslims coming to live in our free Western societies need to know how we got our freedoms. Our freedoms exist because—beginning long ago and increasingly over time—we stopped tolerating fraud, murder and injustice in politics and, yes, even in religion. Mohammed and the Koran are sancrosanct in Mecca, but not in Madrid or Minneapolis. It is high time for free people everywhere to let Muslims know what we think about their implausible book and their wretch of a "prophet."

Confront Muslim acquaintances frankly. Show them the facts plainly. If sufficient numbers of people do this over time—not in harangues, but in the context of respectful day-to-day conversation—naive Muslims will eventually realize that they owe it to themselves to examine the Koran more closely. Then they will see for themselves what we see. Surely then they will begin to *think* for themselves. Some will feel a natural revulsion of conscience.

What if they are *not* repulsed? What if they prefer the Koran in spite of its violence and pseudomorality? At least, in that event, they will know why we do not join them, why we honor them but not their religion and why we do not vote their leaders into public office. If hearing their purportedly holy book decanonized is too stressful for some Muslims, perhaps they will decide not to live where people refuse to blindly submit, submit, submit. No free society can ever be a comforting environment for unquestioning submitters.

So—plead earnestly. Reason patiently. Welcome Muslims to your neighborhoods and into your homes. Rejoice over them if they forsake Islam. Never threaten or insult them, no matter how angrily they respond.

If they repulse you, remember the 200-year-old maxim "It is hard to reason a person out of something that he did not reason himself into."

A friend of mine said, "Islam is waging war on us. Let's wage peace on Islam." I prefer to say, "Let's wage *truth* on Islam—because truth is the doorway to genuine peace. Peace not founded upon truth cannot last."

Never threaten or insult Muslims, no matter how angrily they respond.

Readers who wish to respond with comments, queries and/or suggestions for our future as Westerners sharing a world with Muslims may e-mail me at:

TheKoranExaminer@AOL.com

Responses will be categorized. Stats on opinions expressed will be published periodically on my website:

www.DonRichardsonBookSales.com

Responses which evidence that the responder is unfamiliar with the content of this book will not be categorized. Responses must include your name, city and state and be no longer than one computer screenful.

Readers may also peruse and order books on Islam—including many quoted in the text of this book—at discounted prices from the same website.

God bless us all with peace based upon *His* principles. May He deliver the entire world from the jihadic pseudopeace that comes through submission to Mohammed.

As Sir William Muir wrote:

The sword of Mahomet [Mohammed] and the Coran [Koran] are the most stubborn enemies of civilization, liberty, and truth that the world has yet known.[1]

French philologist Ernest Renan echoes: "Muslims are the first victims of Islam. . . . To liberate a Muslim from his religion is the best service that one can render him."[2]

Triumphing over that enemy without becoming like that enemy in the process is surely mankind's ultimate challenge.

Notes

1. William Muir, *The Life of Muhammad* (Edinburgh, United Kingdom: T. & T. Clark, 1923), n.p.
2. Ernest Renan, quoted in Ibn Warraq, *Why I Am Not a Muslim* (Amherst, NY: Prometheus Books, 1995), n.p.

THE KORAN'S 109 WAR VERSES

On the next page are the 109 verses
found in Dawood's translation of the Koran. Verses that
mention war in storytelling (e.g. "David slew Goliath" in 2:251)
are not included. Nor are verses in which "God" afflicts
infidels—*if Muslims did not help him!*

THE KORAN'S 109 WAR VERSES

2:178	4:71	8:5	9:5	16:110	63:4
179	72	7	12		
190	74	9	13	22:39	64:14
191	75	12	14	78	
193	76	15	16		66:9
216	77	16	19	29:6	
217	84	17	20	69	73:20
218	89	39	24		
244	91	42	25	33:7	
	94	45	26	18	
3:121	95	59	29	20	
122	100	65	36	25	
123	102	67	38	26	
124	104	69	39		
125		71	41	47:20	
140	5:33	72	44		
155	35	74	52	48:16	
165	38	75	73	22	
166			81		
167			83	59:2	
169			86	5	
173			88	6	
195			92	7	
			111	8	
			120	14	
			122		
			123	60:9	
				61:4	

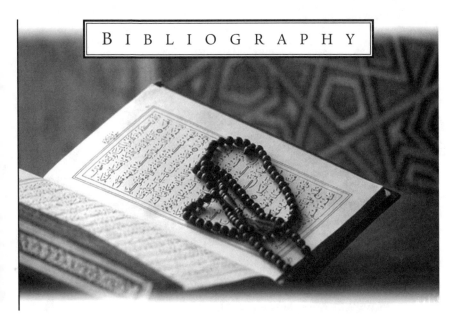

BIBLIOGRAPHY

Armstrong, Karen. *Muhammad, A Biography of the Prophet.* New York: HarperCollins, 1992. Note: Not recommended.

Cati, W. L. *Married to Mohammed: One Woman's Marriage to a Muslim and His Religion.* Lake Mary, FL: Creation House, 2001.

Gabriel, Mark A. *Islam and Terrorism.* Lake Mary, FL: Charisma House, 2002.

Goodwin, Jan. *Price of Honor: Muslim Women Lift the Veil of Silence on the Islamic World.* London: Warner Books, 1998. Note: Goodwin reports a plethora of cruelty to Muslim women but backs away from faulting Mohammed and the Koran for Islam's antifemale outrages. Abhorring the symptoms, she absolves the disease.

Lewis, Bernard. *Islam in History: Ideas, People and Events in the Middle East.* Chicago: Open Court Publishing, 1993.

Mahmoody, Betty, with William Hoffer. *Not Without My Daughter.* New York: St. Martins Press, 1987.

Muir, William. *The Life of Muhammad.* Edinburgh, United Kingdom: T. & T. Clark, 1923.

Musk, Bill. *The Unseen Face of Islam.* Eastbourne, Great Britain: MARC, 1989.

Pipes, Daniel. *Militant Islam Reaches America.* New York: W.W. Norton and Company, 2002.

Price, Randall. *Unholy War: America, Israel and Radical Islam.* Eugene, OR: Harvest House, 2001.

Pryce-Jones, David. *The Closed Circle: An Interpretation of the Arabs.* New York: HarperCollins, 1991.

Rodinson, Maxime. *Muhammad.* New York: Pantheon Books, 1971.

Safa, Reza F. *Inside Islam: Exposing and Reaching the World of Islam.* Lake Mary, FL: Creation House, 1997.

Sasson, Jean. *Daughters of Arabia.* London: Bantam Books, 1997.

Sasson, Jean P. *Princess.* New York: Avon Books, 1992.

Ye'or, Bat. *Islam and Dhimmitude: Where Civilizations Collide.* Cranbury, NJ: Associated University Presses, 2002.

Warraq, Ibn. *Why I Am Not a Muslim.* Amherst, NY: Prometheus Books, 1995.

INDEX

More of the Best from Don Richardson

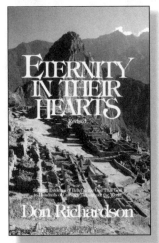
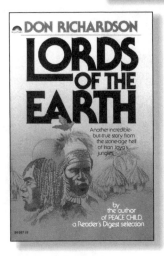
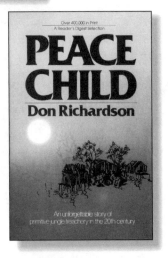

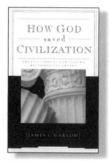

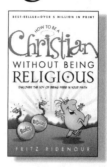

For these and other books, videos and DVDs, visit www.donrichardsonbooksales.com

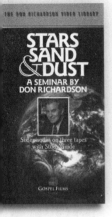

Stars, Sand & Dust: A Seminar by Don Richardson

God promised Abraham, Isaac and Jacob that their descendants—both physical and spiritual—would be as numerous as the STARS in the sky, the SAND on the seashore and the DUST of the earth.

Don Richardson traces that foundational promise, showing that the vast majority of those descendants will be Gentiles, drawn by the Gospel from "every language, tribe, people and nation."

VHS—Six 45-minute episodes on three tapes
Includes Study Guide

Peace Child: The Classic, True Missionary Drama

Don and Carol Richardson respond to the call of Christ. Careful preparation for their mission and a journey by dug-out canoe bring them to a remote rain forest inhabited by some of the world's most primitive people. Painstakingly, they learn the language only to be shocked when the story of Judas' betrayal of Jesus makes him a hero to a people whose highest attribute is to be masters of treachery.

When inter-tribal warfare breaks out, the battles continue until a warring chief offers his son as a means of bringing lasting peace. This primitive tribal custom makes the Gospel understandable. Lives are changed. A church appears.

VHS/DVD—30 minutes
DVD has 17 laguages on one disc!

Candle In the Dark: The Story of William Carey

He sailed in 1793 to India with a reluctant wife and four children to bring the message of Jesus. There he encountered so much hardship it is amazing he didn't abandon his mission and go home. But he stayed for over 40 years.

One issue that tormented him was *sati*—the burning alive of widows when their husbands died. Facing insurmountable odds, he "plodded" on to influence the abolition of *sati* and to become the revered "Friend of India" and "Father of Modern Missions."

Carey's legacy has inspired countless others from his own day to the present. He shows dramatically how a life dedicated to God and obedient to His calling can make a profound difference in the world.

VHS—97 minutes

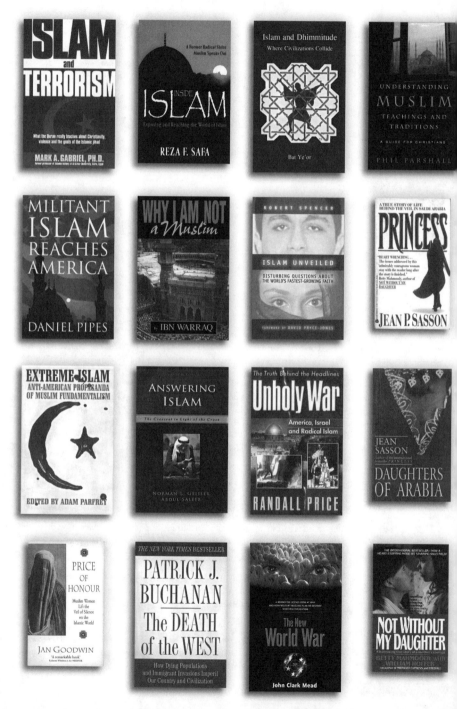